UNITY and Beyond

UNITY

—AND—

BEYOND

FIVE SIMPLE STEPS TO STOP
LETTING CONFLICT WIN

BRANDON
BIGELOW

MDR, MPA, LNHA, & CEO OF FUSION CONFLICT STRATEGIES

UNITY AND BEYOND
Five Simple Steps to Stop Lettng Conflict Win

Copyright © 2026 by Brandon Bigelow

Book Cover Design by Alex Kirkland
Interior Layout and Design by Stephanie Anderson
Editorial Team: Greg Spielberg, Marcie Taylor, Tessa Carvalho

ISBNs:
979-8-89165-371-9 *Paperback*
979-8-89165-372-6 *Hardcover*
979-8-89165-370-2 *E-book*

Published by:
Streamline Books
Kansas City, MO
shareyourstory.com

STREAMLINE BOOKS

To my always and forever, Kathryn, who has never waned in her belief that I was capable of far more than I ever imagined!

CONTENTS

INTRODUCTION

Somewhere in the Great Plains, the wind whips mightily. Gray clouds begin to roll in, and thunder rumbles in the distance. Herds of cattle, lifting their heads mid-graze, recognize that a storm is approaching and begin moving in the opposite direction—*away* from the impending lightning, the straight-line gusts, nature's nourishing chaos.

But the American Bison? They also run, but it is *toward* that storm. *Toward* that chaos.

Both the fleeing cattle and the charging buffalo have the same instinctive goal: self-preservation, safety, comfort, survival. But their approaches and their outcomes could not be more different.

The truth? The cattle will never fully outrun the danger that stretches for miles, and by fleeing, they ensure that they will spend *more* time in these conditions, essentially traveling with the storm as it chases them.

The bison, on the other hand, will experience discomfort in the beginning of their journey when they meet the storm, but they know that beyond the edges of those cranky clouds is drier weather. Safety. A more peaceful day on the plains—if only they can get through the tough part first.

As humans, there is much we can learn from the behavior of the cattle and the buffalo, especially as it relates to conflict. When we feel a storm approaching (or even if we're already drenched)—storms such as interpersonal disagreements at work that halt growth and progress, trouble collaborating on teams and making decisions, and even challenges in our personal lives—we would do well to behave like the buffalo, moving toward drier weather and calmer skies even if it means facing the rain first.

This book will teach you how.

The UNITY Promise

UNITY is a conflict resolution framework like no other because it recognizes a core truth: Conflict is only about 5 percent issue-driven and roughly 95 percent emotionally driven. (Yep, even conflict at work!) UNITY takes that dynamic not just loosely into consideration but rather centers it as a necessary factor—one directly related to outcomes and my experience of conflict resolution as a whole.

Together in this book, I will take you through each step and illustrate not just the how, but the deeper why that makes this process so effective.

- **Unpack** prior individual biases, notions, and suppositions of your own—and those of the other party with whom you're in conflict.
- **Navigate** where the other party might be coming from in terms of their position and potential biases, working to understand their likely motivations without agreeing or disagreeing.
- **Identify** commonalities with which you both agree as a fruitful place to begin.

- **Take Ownership** for your own part by initiating a conversation and committing to being more open minded, keeping an open dialogue, and being willing to see through other lenses.
- **Yield** to new possibilities that will come your way as you accept the differences in others that you can't change and instead focus on forging ahead in UNITY.

I know what you might be thinking: *Wait, so practicing UNITY means I need to put aside my opinions and feelings? It means I need to defer by default?*

No, not exactly. In fact, practicing UNITY invariably leads to better and faster outcomes than if conflict had escalated with heels dug in.

Instead of looking at conflict in a binary way of "win or lose," "right or wrong," the goal of UNITY is to arrive at middle ground. From this middle ground, we don't need to lose sight of our position, but we focus more on commonalities and leading with empathy. Despite what you may know of conflict to this point, it *is* possible for all parties involved to walk away feeling seen, respected, and heard, even if disagreements run deep. After that foundation of empathy and trust is built, that embedded understanding and recognition of another's humanity can even ward off future disagreements, leading to not just higher productivity but better relationships overall—and that's where the magic happens. An empathetic and trusting team can lead to higher employee retention and better metrics across the board. But besides those benefits, there are other positive outcomes at play.

Solving conflict is not your only goal. There are bigger questions to consider: Do you desire a life well lived? Do you wish to travel a peaceful road ahead, with the confidence that no matter what situation you may face, no matter how dire the circumstances and how dark the days are in front of you, you'll have the mindset and knowledge to resolve life's setbacks at advanced levels and be a conduit for others to do the same? No matter your family dynamics or the details of your job, you'll be more effectual and will develop greater peace and tranquility with who you are as a person. You will ultimately achieve a more profound sense of commitment with the ways in which you interact and overcome differences with others in your everyday life.

The UNITY process brings people together. It gives you the energy and ability to draw individuals and groups to your cause. Yes, as a manager, you can help resolve the conflict between two team members, but it's fundamentally so much greater than that.

If you're tired of not making progress when it comes to conflict resolution, no matter how many different approaches you may have tried in the past, I have good news: UNITY starts from within and ripples outward to everyone with whom you interact. When you are willing to make a course correction and finally come to the table of new and fresh approaches to mitigating disputes through the UNITY framework, I believe you'll find that the greatest source of success is for you and everyone else around you to achieve results *together* in the most connected, enlightened, and amicable way possible. UNITY is the new way forward. It's a self-initiated, self-driven process that addresses the matter at hand while also vastly improving the broader landscape. With an effective, sustainable approach to taking charge of conflict, you and those with whom you interact can be much more successful, feeling the kind of true happiness that occurs when you've achieved significant things together. Through UNITY, we can redefine success as a process that unfolds collectively and benefits all involved, not just a select few and not only an organization's bottom line.

If you think dispute resolution is just about resolving day-to-day conflict, this journey has something so much bigger in store. First, you draw success from deep within yourself, and then you progress to the next level of drawing it from others. When that happens, it's a beautiful symmetry and breathtaking dance that leads to results you previously didn't think were possible. It's so much more than "checking a box."

Plenty of books talk about teamwork and cheerlead the notion of working together. That's different from going straight to the root and addressing the most toxic types of conflict in organizations and in families. Often, the most supportive allies in your success start out as the people with whom you have the greatest conflict, because they're just as passionate as you are. If that fervor is tilted to the negative, you'll be butting heads—but at least you know you both care. You have skin in the game and feel strongly. Those people make great partners because once you can understand each other and achieve symbioses, you don't need to drag the other party along. They're already highly motivated. If you've proven you're willing to do the work, the other party will often meet you in the middle, and together, you can achieve mutual enlightenment and understanding that you didn't think possible.

That's why UNITY is worth the investment—not just because it's the right thing to do when you're in conflict. It can also help you achieve a synergistic state on a level that had previously been out of reach.

When UNITY Works

Conflict exists on a continuum, and UNITY works across that continuum.

Left unaddressed, conflict can become toxic, leading to a breakdown in collaboration and, in certain circumstances, even litigation or other extremely consequential actions. UNITY bridges divides early, like between two coworkers who need to collaborate on a project but don't see eye to eye. When people lack critical skills to communicate effectively, those differences of opinion can slow progress and cause deliverables to suffer. UNITY is an essential toolkit when opinions differ and, instead of passing judgment or driving people apart, finds ways to successfully work together and believe it or not… actually enjoy it!

Sometimes, with people who have collaborated on projects or have been in personal relationships for a period of time, festering frustrations about personality conflicts can go unresolved. If they lack the basic skills necessary to effectively communicate, there sometimes is a tendency to entertain or even initiate gossip, hearsay, or speculation about the other party. And, of course, all too often, this reality may eventually lead to a contentious or even hostile environment, which can cause irreparable harm with whatever shred of morale that may still remain.

There are also more serious issues of harassment that arise as HR allegations. When you have an accusation and still have the ability to resolve it internally, UNITY can work to surface the challenges that led to the issue and seek mutual solutions.

When individual harassment issues become par for the course, organizations can end up with a toxic culture on the verge of implosion. At that point, leadership is usually desperate to figure out what went wrong and shift immediately to make changes. Of course, it's better to prevent those systemic challenges from forming in the first place, but if you've reached that point, UNITY can help there too. If you adopt it early, it can be a preventive tool. When teams have these skills from the beginning, conflicts are much less likely to escalate to litigation.

Discovering Calling Through Conflict

I've been in the healthcare industry for many years, leading numerous organizations large and small. Early in my career, though, I took a detour. At the time, my dad had a successful manufacturing business, which produced, marketed, and sold ultraviolet lights and self-cleaning technology to HVAC dealers. The dealers then provided this upgrade to their customers' heating and air-conditioning equipment. This provided a huge benefit by eliminating airborne pathogens while increasing overall efficiency. It was the early 2000s, and this new technology was just beginning to take hold.

As my Dad's company began to scale more quickly, he asked if I'd be interested in working together to help run operations and marketing. My brother, Curtis, was also working with the company at the time and oversaw accounting and finances. My role would be to help build the brand through expansion with increased marketing and distribution channels. After giving the offer a great deal of thought and prayer, I decided that working with my dad—a man whom I've spent a lifetime admiring and striving to emulate—would be a wonderful opportunity.

The thought of being able to pick his brain on the daily and learn from someone who had been in the trenches, teaching, authoring books, consulting, and partnering with business owners and executives in their quest for operational and business excellence, stayed with me, and I couldn't shake it. For as long as I can remember, I'd hoped to eventually be half the business leader with maybe a quarter of the brainpower as my father. This seemed like the perfect opportunity to truly tap into that desire with my dad.

I thought the job would just be for a short time, maybe a year. I wanted to get away from the negative work environment I was in at the time, so I took the chance. We accomplished some meaningful work together. I helped my dad grow the business, launched an indoor air quality education division for his current and future dealers, and created a distribution company that provided this ultraviolet technology to West Coast dealers. I had a blast during this time, and it gave me the opportunity to think creatively while away from the healthcare industry.

Even so, I felt a bit conflicted, because I started to realize how much I missed my former role within the senior care space. My dad's business was doing well financially, and the distribution company that I had put together was beginning to take off. Judging by my paycheck, I was successful, but each day I'd look in the mirror and not know who I was serving besides myself and my bank account. Don't get me wrong, those three years working side by side with my dad and brother were very meaningful. We deepened our family relationship and significantly grew the business. But HVACs didn't feel like my calling. I didn't feel that I was helping others as much as I had been in my prior role: supporting the health and welfare needs of the vulnerable, the elderly, and those needing in-patient rehabilitation services. Working a job that didn't feel like a calling started to take its toll.

When we're feeling stuck, it's tempting to assign blame. *Whose fault is it?* Often, though, we need to take a deeper dive to fully appreciate the context and what's happening. Maybe there is an external disagreement, but it starts from a conflict within ourselves. We aren't in the right situation, or we don't have a clear sense of our own priorities. In my case, I was doing a good job with my dad's business, but I wanted something more meaningful than the external validation of a paycheck. As grueling as it was to come to that realization, it was more difficult to picture how to communicate this to my dad. He's always been an exceptionally understanding and empathic person, and I knew he would support my decision to leave. But I felt inner turmoil and guilt walking away from our family business. When I worked up the courage and spoke to him about my decision to leave and to return to my roots in healthcare, he was magnanimous and supportive. "Go find your passion," he said, "and I'll be your biggest cheerleader when you do!" I'm happy to report, he kept his word!

Though a challenging transition, it was a necessary step in my professional journey. I needed the time away to see what mattered and realize what would actually make me feel happy and fulfilled. When I returned to healthcare, I was forced to take a step down in title and compensation. I wasn't starving, but I had to eat crow. I think of it as my *Lost in America* moment, after the eighties movie in which a couple drops out of corporate society and tries to make it on their own, only to end up groveling to return. But that didn't stop me.

When I returned, I was on fire. That renewed commitment allowed me to harness a new vision to help other healthcare operations transform. Being unhappy and settling that conflict within myself lit the spark for me to pursue my core purpose from then on, and it's taken me many places—including ultimately cofounding Fusion Conflict Strategies, LLC, where I've been blessed to have helped multiple companies and individuals address conflict through the UNITY framework. Our goal in facilitating isn't to handhold on an indefinite contract; we want to be so valuable that eventually we are not needed, that people and teams are empowered with the skills they need to resolve conflicts themselves.

And now, I get to share UNITY with you. How lucky can one guy get?

UNITY Breaks Down Walls

Before we start this journey, I want to tell you a story that embodies the power of UNITY.

Missionary work, and dedicating eighteen months to two years toward a mission, is a big deal in my church. My family and I are invested: My daughter Corinne served in Idaho, Camille is currently serving in Arizona, my daughter-in-law, Whitney, served in Korea, and our daughter Natalie chose to marry her soulmate Luke before she was able to serve (and we're thrilled she found her person!). My sons have been equally motivated in service to their Maker. Jared served his mission in Korea, Will in Argentina, my son-in-law, Sam, served in New England, my other son-in-law, Luke, in Chile, and my youngest, Reid, will have the opportunity to serve in the coming years. In my case, when I was nineteen, my mission was based in Jacksonville, serving northern Florida and southern Georgia. I received three weeks of training in Provo, Utah, before heading out. Those learning a new language—like my cousin who served in Berlin—trained for longer.

It was early November 1989 when my cousin was getting ready for his assignment to Berlin, and as it turned out, we were both training for our respective assignments in Provo at the same time. If you're a history buff like me, you'll recall that the Berlin Wall fell on November 9, 1989 . . . exactly one day after I entered full-time missionary service. This mammoth world event was a powerful symbol that led to a series of historical turning points that exposed Soviet and communist shortcomings.

The toppling of the wall that separated East and West Germany since 1961, along with Soviet leader Mikhail Gorbachev's reform efforts to loosen the tight grip of Communism in Eastern Europe, set into motion the eventual fall of the Soviet Union and allowed for the whole of Eastern Europe to become independent and free. At the missionary training center, we were in a bubble, unaware of the outside world. We didn't watch TV or go to the movies; we were just with our mission companions, full-time, twenty-four hours a day. It's a feeling not unlike the military, pushing personal growth and creating a world unto itself for a period of time.

Then, just as I was settling into the end of my first full day in this spiritual cocoon, I heard the blessed news, from one of my instructors, about the miracle of this wall coming down; the wall that had been a literal dividing line between democracy and communism for nearly three decades. The country unified just when we became sequestered from the outside world.

The Berlin Wall toppling down opened up East Germany not just to more freedom but also to missionaries from different faiths all around the world. My cousin and I were in completely different groups on the grounds of the Missionary Training Center, but I couldn't wait to find him to tell him the news. It took me a few hours to track him down. "Steven," I said, "can you believe what's happening?" We embraced, and he was emotional. He clearly had heard the same news and was overcome with joy. His excitement level was elevated because he knew he could serve people more deeply and profoundly for the next two years than he'd ever imagined. The world was opening up and changing right before our eyes.

This story—and this book—is not about religion or missionaries proselyting to the world. It is, however, about the magic of that moment and being able to recreate it in our own circumstances. If we're lucky, our lives have a handful of those extraordinary events that reveal our deeper purpose. That was one of mine—and of Steven's. As I've continued to develop and train people on the UNITY framework, I've felt the metaphorical walls come down too. It opens opportunities for shared joy, new possibilities, and—the biggest value proposition of all—connection.

What to Expect in This Book

There is no such thing as a life on the Plains free from its legendary thunderstorms, just like there is no such thing as a life free from conflict. And like the buffalo, we can boldly face these situations head on, if we have a path.

As we move forward together, we'll start by addressing the roots of conflict, answering questions like: How did we get here, and what psychological considerations are at play when we're in conflict with ourselves, others, or systems/organizations? Is all conflict "bad"? How do we know when something needs to be addressed and when it can be left alone? And so much more.

From there, we'll explore UNITY in detail, moving through each step—*unpack, navigate, identify, take ownership,* and *yield*—in great detail. You'll learn why each step (and its sequence) matters, how to apply the principle to your specific situation in the "Put It into Practice" sections, and what pitfalls and opportunities to look for along the way.

At the end of our time together, once you've learned not just to address conflict in a healthy way but also to help others do the same, you'll know how to create environments where people do great work *and* feel happy doing it.

And by people, I mean *you* too. UNITY will empower you to handle the storms, give you confidence to solve problems with compassion and spot whispers of thunderclouds on the horizon much sooner than before. Your business outcomes will improve, sure . . . but after fully embracing UNITY, you'll see that's just, in reality, the proverbial cherry on top.

Ready? Let's get started.

CHAPTER 1

The Roots of Conflict: How We Got Here

Though I didn't seek out conflicts, from an early age, I seemed to have no problems finding them. The San Francisco Bay Area where I lived in the 1970s and early 1980s was a far cry from what it resembles today. I was raised in an upper-middle-class family by supportive parents. And when I say supportive, I mean they pretty much let me do whatever I was up for, pretty much anytime I was up for it.

In an era where smartphones were only something imagined on episodes of *The Jetsons,* it was not just common but expected as a kid that the minute that I returned home from school, I was on my bike and off to the baseball diamond, Thrifty's for ice cream, or down to the creek near my house in search of polliwogs, small frogs, and other slimy amphibious creatures. It was a time like no other. Idyllic doesn't come close to articulating what I experienced in my own "age of innocence."

My earliest memory involving what could be deemed as some element of conflict occurred when I was nine. My friend Emery, who lived seven houses down on the opposite side of the street, ventured over to my house one Saturday evening in the summer of 1980. We bantered about a series of schemes that involved everything from hitchhiking to the new state-of-the-art Stoneridge Mall to building a sailboat out of logs, rope, and bedsheets and launching off the dock at Lake Del Valle. After an exhaustive discussion, we eventually decided that the logistics involved in these adventures were probably way more daunting than two boys, just short of adolescence, should ever dare to undertake. I didn't know a lot in 1980, but at least I had a vague notion of what *I actually didn't know.*

Forty-five years removed, I honestly don't recall whose idea came next, but our wisdom in foregoing the first two terrible Saturday-night activities definitely did not extend to what was decided next. One of us (I'm going to go ahead and say it was most likely Emery) came up with the brilliant notion that what the houses on our street needed most was a good old-fashioned "doorbell ditching." Our neighborhood of homes on Hummingbird Lane, built in the late sixties, was mostly middle- to upper-middle-class families, and experienced little to no neighborhood kid "shenanigans." That means what was surely considered a benign Saturday-night activity in many other areas would likely be looked upon as a serious breach in neighborly trust, behavior, and decorum.

It began easily enough. A fairly simple plan was hatched where Emery and I alternated between the ringer and the runner. I remember not feeling as bad when I was only the runner. After studying law in college (and listening to my fair share of true crime podcasts over the years), I now know that the "lookout" or "runner" or "getaway driver," whatever the complementary offense might be, can be treated just as harshly as the offender.

But I was a kid then, and all I wanted? To be the runner.

After several successful covert ops on Hummingbird Lane, we felt unstoppable and emboldened. In the days before video doorbells, we judged our success by the homeowner's suspicious, futile, confused glances up and down the street. From our hiding spots, ducking down near front-yard hedges or behind a large Ford Econoline van, we could easily size up the depth of the victim's efforts to spot us. We had insatiable glee as each of them quickly gave up the fight.

In retrospect, we thought it was our clever choice of neighborhood hideaways, but in reality, the fact that we began at dusk and continued well after dark surely played the biggest role. Whatever it was that escalated our confidence in those moments on that evening, it provided the spark in seeking the ultimate prize: to successfully doorbell ditch the Green family, who lived four doors down from my house. Mr. Green, or "Old Man Green" as we called him, didn't seem capable of being anything but the meanest and scariest neighbor there ever was. Nobody, and I mean nobody, could convince me to the contrary. And unfortunately for Emery and myself, on that summer night so many years ago, we definitely "fooled around and found out."

Neither of us admitted out loud to each other the two most obvious realities as we approached Old Man Green's house. Number one, each of us desperately wanted to act in the role of "runner" rather than "ringer" in this uniquely terrifying moment. And number two, we both knew that if we were caught in this instance, we would never live to see puberty. After three successive "rock, paper, scissors" challenges, I was the unfortunate soul who landed the role of ringer. (Emery's instincts were always better than mine, and it was never more obvious than that Saturday night.)

So with every ounce of courage I could muster from my slight "five-foot-nothing, a hundred-and-nothing-pound" frame, with my heart beating out of my chest, I slowly sauntered toward the front door. I've forgotten a lot about that night, but I vividly recall that despite every ounce of strength I could muster to prevent my left hand and arm from shaking, I could barely aim my index finger anywhere near the small button. Finally, I used my right hand to guide my finger to the target.

It wasn't the traditional "ding dong" sound . . . this was that loud, triumphant chime that had a total of eight deafening and distinct notes.

What occurred next is a bit of a blur. I turned to run toward my house, which was the direction I thought Emery was also running. But he had the jitters too. Rather than running past three houses and then escaping through my family's side gate, Emery jumped into my next-door neighbor's hedges and, as I ran past, reached out and pulled me into his dubious lair. Before I could get us to freedom, Old Man Green's front door slammed shut so hard, we were shocked his windows didn't shatter.

"I don't know who you are or where you're hiding, but I'm coming for you! And it's not going to be pretty," Old Man Green yelled, channeling his inner Liam Neeson, decades before *Taken*. It was terrifying in only the way one experiences a true belief that they are about to be beaten to an inch of their life . . . or worse. Reflecting for decades on this experience, I honestly couldn't tell you whether the pause between his blood-curdling howl and what happened next took five seconds or five minutes. Time truly stood still that cool July night, and my sense of reality was shattered.

My memory gets foggy from there. There are a smattering of images and dialogue that vaguely come back to me if I really allow myself to go there. I recall getting marched through Old Man Green's front door, through his entryway, and straight onto his mint-green upholstered couch. I could easily be convinced that I spent the next three hours under interrogation in that random living room on Hummingbird Lane. I could also just as easily believe that I was grilled by this tyrant for just north of five minutes. However, what is absolutely seared into my brain were two very direct and threatening statements: "We just had vandalism occur at our house last week, and I think you two were responsible for every bit of it," and "I've already called the police. They're on their way!"

While I couldn't be sure if he truly believed we vandalized his home, police officers did indeed arrive to scare the ever-loving crap out of two terrified ten-year-olds.

The events of that evening four decades ago were one of my very earliest memories of conflict. It wasn't subtle. It wasn't cagey. It was an assault on all of my senses and introduced me to the power dynamics issues that impact every ounce of division, debate, and disharmony.

Now, I realize the incident with Old Man Green is a very specific memory of a very distinct type of conflict—one I initiated through my own actions, surely, as a thrill-seeking adolescent. You're not necessarily coming to this book because you want to be able to handle the "Old Man Green" in your life. I'm guessing you're here for a bunch of different reasons. However, if each of us look back far enough, we will most likely discover an experience or two that shook us in such a significant way that we consciously or unconsciously decided that we wanted to find something, anything, to deal with the painful and uncomfortable process of responding to all of the deep emotional turmoil that came along with that experience.

The truth is that conflict comes in all shapes and sizes, and despite its broad nature, there are some common signs of toxicity in relationships and in organizations: lack of communication, fear of honesty, possessiveness, lack of motivation and connection, failure to collaborate effectively, doing "the right thing" for optics sake . . . I could go on, and on, and on.

Toxic environments can be explicit or implicit, but however you look at it, a house built on sand—one built in conflict—will not stand. That's a lonely place to be. Our bodies remember that feeling too . . . of increased heart rate, of frustration physically manifesting, of feeling scared or silenced or exasperated or any other array of negative feelings or emotions.

That's why I told you about an obscure story of my daunting experience with Old Man Green even though I know doorbell ditching isn't necessarily on your bingo card anytime soon. It's because you have that moment in you, too, I'll bet. A conflict you can remember, one that lives in the recesses of your memories. One that changed how you operate in the world today. My goal in writing this is that when faced with your next conflict, you'll be vastly better equipped. No more ducking into the proverbial bushes.

But before we can talk about equipping you with the UNITY process, we must first understand the nature of conflict in the first place, including the role of the ego.

The Psychology of Conflict and Ego

Not all conflict is bad. Not by a long shot.

Read that again if you have to.

In fact, healthy conflict can be constructive, can stimulate innovation, deepen relationships, and learning. On the other hand, unhealthy conflict tends to be destructive, eroding trust, collaboration, and well-being.

Both internal and external factors interact dynamically. For example, a stressed organizational climate (external) may trigger anxiety in a conflict-averse employee (internal), creating a cycle of avoidance and miscommunication. Many times, the ego comes into play here.

Let me give you an example. When I started my career, I worked for a man named Dick. He hired me from among a couple dozen candidates, seemingly because he sensed that he could take me under his wing. I was fresh out of college with a BS in political science and a minor in economics. Given my education and background, I had no business going into healthcare. I saw the role as something like an MBA where I could learn about management.

I was young, hungry, and impressionable. In my appreciation for Dick's mentorship, I put way too much stock into every word he said. Soon, he began driving me around to various nursing home operations under his command, walking the premises, pointing out issues, and berating people in a very outward, public way.

Afterward, he would ask, "What did I do in that situation?" The funny thing is, he never said, "What did I do *wrong?*" In retrospect, I could not find anything all these years later that he did right. He took me to about five to six different operations in central California, and it was the same everywhere he went: People cowered in fear. He was my "assigned" mentor, so I believed that I had no choice but to adopt his various approaches, even though most of them felt highly unnatural. He would often say, "Do you see how I interact with my people and why I'm so successful? I've been doing this for decades, and they all know how I am." He made the conflict seem natural, almost inevitable at times, and definitely part of my job. In essence, the message was clear: If I wanted to succeed at the highest levels like Dick had, I needed to show my staff who was in charge by "showing" everyone outwardly who was in charge.

Dick's philosophy reminded me of Michael Douglas's character, Gordon Gecko, in *Wall Street*, who says, "The point is, ladies and gentleman, that greed, for the lack of a better word, is good. Greed is right, greed works. Greed clarifies, cuts through, and captures the essence of the evolutionary spirit." If you replace "greed" with "conflict," that was Dick.

He used to advise me, "You want to stir things up, because if they're exactly as they are, then you'll never see results." To some extent, he was right; sometimes you do need to shake things up in order to reach higher operational plains. However, he exhibited his approaches in a way that vastly miscalculated the negative impact on those who reported to him and completely underestimated the long-term damage caused to these critical employees. He had some extremely talented people who worked for him, including Julianne (whom I will talk more about later in this chapter).

After I received my nursing home administrator's license, a building opened up, and Dick gave me my first opportunity to lead. Even though you can probably tell that I wasn't wild about his approaches, I will always be grateful that he clearly saw something in me that I didn't see in myself and ultimately gave me my start in the wild and wonderful career in healthcare operations.

I went to work immediately, implementing what I'd learned up to that point: Dick's management playbook. It did not go well. The staff knew that I seemed "off," and this reality wasn't lost on me for a moment. Fortunately, I had some managers whom I oversaw who very kindly and very bravely told me that what I was doing was not working. Rather than being more self-aware of the messaging that they were attempting to provide me, I didn't fully connect the dots until they approached me. It took those fiercely honest and dedicated professionals to eventually get me back on track. To this day, I admire their guts, because this was an early observation, and they didn't know me from Adam. All they knew was I had an aggressive management and communication style, and it didn't serve their departments or our entire organization in any positive way.

One of them said, rightly, "This doesn't seem like who you are." That statement hit me between the eyes. They could sense that I was playing a role instead of being my authentic self, that my ego was winning. To clarify, I've never considered myself to have a large ego. But in my sophomoric approach to my leadership role in those early years, I told myself that being in charge automatically meant my employees respected me.

To their credit, they didn't say, "Hey, stop acting that way, or we're going to quit." Instead, they held up a metaphorical mirror and showed me I was betraying my real self and purpose. In my three decades of experience, I've come to learn that when you consent to work for someone, even for a short time, you quickly figure out whether they're playing a part. These brave souls saw that falseness in me and called me out for it. I will forever be grateful for their courage to speak their truths!

At first, I felt offended and embarrassed, so I resisted them. I told them they were wrong. I felt taken back and deeply ashamed. Those feelings turned into a gift, because they led to soul-searching for many days and nights to come.

Those employees technically had less power in the organization than I did. Had they been working for someone like Dick, he would have fired them the next day. To their credit, they saw something in me that wasn't organic, and they took the risk. The more I think about their choice, the more impressed I am. Sometimes the right thing to do doesn't feel safe. Though I was angry at first, I took a step back and reflected. It would be a long time before I developed UNITY, but the seeds were being planted.

In hindsight, I can't believe, let alone condone, how I acted. It was a version of myself I'm not proud of. Having had the experience of acting so unprofessional gives me an understanding of how well-meaning people without the right skills can handle conflict poorly, to the detriment of others and a group's culture. My negative object lesson helped me uncover what works instead—and how to quiet the role of the ego for the greater good.

Two Uncomfortable Truths About Conflict

Naming uncomfortable truths can help us go further, faster. In that spirit, let's unpack two fundamental truths about conflict:

Truth number one: Conflict almost always starts with a communication breakdown, and power dynamics can complicate things. For instance, after thirty-two years, my wife and I have no problem saying to each other, "Hey, you're doing this. It's bothering me." But it can feel less comfortable to speak up at work, particularly if the issue is with someone to whom we report. Power dynamics complicate the situation, to say the least. Even if you're lateral colleagues, people still often shrink away from having direct conversations about what's troubling them at work.

There may be less psychological safety and interpersonal trust in a professional setting. We may fear if we show vulnerability, the other person will take advantage or throw us under the bus. That's why it was such a gift early on when my team took the brave step of flagging my negative behavior.

Truth number two: A certain amount of conflict is inevitable, and we need to accept it. However, when conflict becomes problematic—when it harms business or ruptures close relationships—we need to address it. Conflict in your personal life can spill over to your professional world and vice versa. That's something we all experience, directly or indirectly

Recently, I experienced an internal conflict that rippled beyond the issue at hand. College football is extremely important to my family—my son Reid and I even have a YouTube channel all about our favorite college football team and conference . . . Go Utes! I was trying to buy tickets to an away game to do something special with my wife and two of our boys over Thanksgiving weekend. And this wasn't just any "away game," it was THE GAME . . . Ohio State versus Michigan at "The Big House" in Ann Arbor. I planned ahead and secured a priority slot to buy tickets three months before the game. However, when I logged in, the game was already sold out . . . by 6 a.m. When I reached out to third-party vendors, I had to try four different companies because I received continuous fraud alerts on my credit card. It took me three and a half hours to get the tickets, and by the time I got to work, I was frazzled. It wasn't a relationship-driven conflict; it was just a frustrating experience that had lingering effects on my day and ability to perform. Some primal caveman part of me felt like I'd tried to go hunt for my family and come up short.

How much more profound is that hangover effect when you're having an issue with your spouse, significant other, child, or coworker? From my experience, it's not realistic to leave a conflict at home or at the office; it always seems to spill over in some impactful way.

We'd do well to recognize that all disputes create some level of distraction and deficiency in other aspects of our lives. In the grand scheme, my ticket-buying issue was minute, but it nevertheless derailed my day. Of course, I wouldn't use the UNITY process for a credit-card issue, but the experience reminded me of the importance of tending to our own sense of peace and equilibrium in all aspects of our lives. No matter how much you practice, the journey never ends.

When deciding whether a conflict rises to the level of initiating the UNITY process, simply ask yourself if it's impacting interpersonal relationships or organizational health on any level, however minimal. If the answer is yes, it's completely appropriate to consider following the steps. If something is impacting you negatively, it's likely affecting the relationships around you too.

How Conflict Hides in Plain Sight (and How to Spot It)

Conflict can often hide in plain sight. It can look like staying in your comfort zone, refusing to have uncomfortable and necessary conversations with others. In business, if your bottom line is suffering or you're seeing a high degree of adversity and strife among your team, odds are that conflict has already been embedded within the fabric of your organization.

Conflict can also be masked as "robust debate" or "healthy competition." I've seen this problematic dynamic play out firsthand—and I've even been guilty of giving it ripe conditions in which to grow! Once, when I was overseeing a healthcare operation, I decided to have each of my managers take ownership of different sections of the facility. The intent was solid: to try and have the cleanest areas, the least amount of infection-control issues, the fastest response times when patients pushed their nursing call light . . . you get the picture.

I created an entire scoring system and rubric complete with rewards and prizes for those who separated themselves from the rest of the team. It was going well at first, but the competition eventually turned ugly. I found out some team members were undermining other managers' spaces so they wouldn't score well—the opposite of the purpose of the initiative. As hard as it is to believe that terribly destructive practices like that occur in the name of winning at all costs (see my prior Gordon Gecko *Wall Street* reference for context), it does rear its ugly head. And when it spreads from individuals to whole teams, it can literally take down entire organizations.

It's ironic, isn't it? A cornerstone of UNITY is that it's not about "winning," and in this case, I built a system around precisely that. This goes to show that—even if intentions are good—putting humans into a gamified system can cause behavior change and even disguise conflict if we're not careful.

Masking conflict can also come through mission statements and company values. For example, say you have an organizational mission statement inspired by "optimism." That could mean that at times, when a team member approaches a manager with an issue, rather than give real guidance and resources, that supervisor may just tell the employee to be more *optimistic* and figure out a solution on their own.

Below are some other situations in which conflict can manifest. Note that every company, relationship, and situation is nuanced and different, but odds are you can see yourself and/or your team somewhere in the following common dynamics:

- A struggle with power dynamics. For example: a certified, licensed, or credentialed individual not wanting to take direction from someone who is uncertified, unlicensed, or uncredentialed.
- Trouble with people giving advice to just about everyone else, but not being aware of their own areas for improvement.

- Management's inability to promote strong ideas when they come from employees and instead only validating ideas when they come from executive peers.
- A failure to pick up on conflict in its earliest stages and in some cases actually recognizing that it's rearing its ugly head but making a conscious choice to completely ignore it.
- A tendency to become defensive in the face of criticism—even the constructive kind.
- The presence or threat of significant issues relating to personnel, including potentially even legal action, rumbling like thunder in the distance.

The good news is that once we can recognize these signs, we can take steps to address them with UNITY. I've seen its power firsthand! And when applied the right way, individuals can become masterful at both the recognition and implementation of specific resolution strategies.

Learning From My Calling to Lead

I was once called to a role that showed me what happens when conflict resolution works—the relief, joy, and connection it can bring.

The church in which I am a member, The Church of Jesus Christ of Latter-day Saints, is all volunteer. There's no paid clergy. In 2018, I was asked to serve as a bishop of my congregation, or *ward* as it's known within our religion. This role (or *calling,* as it's referred to) is essentially to act as a leader in all spiritual and temporal affairs of the congregants who attend the ward in which the bishop presides. The role generally lasts about four and a half to five years.

Prior to this call, in the mid 2000s, I served for nearly seven years as one of two counselors to two different bishops in the ward in which

I attended, assisting them with whatever they needed for members and for their own callings. As essentially the "right hand" for these two ward leaders, I'd seen that the role of spiritual leader has many facets, one of which is spiritual counseling. However, as much access as I had to these two different bishops, I eventually realized that I only knew a small part of what they actually did, especially related to assisting individuals, couples, and families who were dealing with personal, relational, and deep spiritual challenges. These were issues that the ward bishop was specifically assigned to address and assist within his role as spiritual leader of his flock.

When I stepped into the role of bishop in January of 2018, I had the responsibility of leading approximately five hundred congregants, taking charge of all meetings, and overseeing all facets of our ward operations. I wore many hats, from marriage therapist to addiction counselor and everything in between.

Relational counseling entailed working with couples who were dealing with serious marital or relationship issues. Although I'd seen the previous bishop provide that support, until I was face-to-face with a couple struggling with pornography or domestic violence and couples on the precipice of divorce, it was hard to fully grasp the gravity of the role. I quickly had to interpret how best to absorb the conflict that they were sharing with me. I frequently prayed for inspiration and guidance. Some members were much older than I was, telling me about their marital issues and asking me for guidance with very sensitive topics.

On one level, I often felt unprepared. Yet I never left those meetings without feeling a sense of peace and calmness. My personal beliefs help me understand why: Each conversation felt daunting, but when I tackled it head on, together, we reached a solution.

From an early age, people have looked to me for guidance through conflict, so by the time I became a bishop, I'd had many opportunities to build that muscle. So many times in my life, circumstances arose that I didn't ask for but needed to find a way through. As the middle child, I often felt thrust into the role of peacemaker, whether I sought it out or not. I learned to navigate the competing interests of both younger and older siblings. As a bishop, I jumped in the deep end again and learned a ton as I went.

People came to me presenting a vast array of challenges, but they usually boiled down to a spiritual or interpersonal relationship. Over time, it became clear to me that relationship development has the power to solve problems. That insight underpins UNITY.

IQ vs. EQ

When facing conflicts in our personal or professional lives, there's often a tendency to approach them from a purely analytical or intelligence quotient (IQ) standpoint. It makes sense: Sometimes, it can feel easier to try and find a logical "fix" rather than do the emotional heavy lifting. The truth is that we need to leverage both IQ and emotional intelligence (EQ) to find long-term, sustainable solutions to complex disagreements.

EQ is the state from which we permit ourselves to be uncomfortable as a mechanism for growth and healing, allowing us to see different perspectives and challenge our own. It is the critical skillset that allows us to break down deep-seated walls of isolation.

Unfortunately, there is no conflict—large or small—that can be repaired with an "aha" moment born of IQ alone. Trying to solve a conflict with IQ only is like trying to put a Band-Aid over a wound that's bleeding profusely; it's simply not going to be enough. True resolution requires that we not only intellectually recognize the "what" but demands that we emotionally discover the "why."

Leading with both IQ and EQ takes effort, certainly. But the most rewarding things in life never come easy, and there is nothing more rewarding than healthy human connection. By proceeding with both IQ and EQ, we can collectively move toward more of that!

Where We Go, Conflict Will Follow

This story is hard for me to talk about without getting a little emotional.

There was a watershed moment for me several years ago that came at an unexpected time and circumstance. After building from the ground up and leading my own healthcare company into exponential growth, I ran headfirst into a brick wall. A combination of negative industry trends and regulatory challenges impacted my business in seriously challenging ways. Despite wanting to stay and fight through all of the chaos, I made a key decision that impacted the rest of my career. I walked away, feeling a deep sense of hurt, anger, and a whole lot of fear of what road lay ahead for me in this transformational moment in time. One of the first things I did was decide that the time was right to explore an arena I'd always wanted to immerse myself in. I ended up applying (and to my great surprise was accepted) to Caruso School of Law at Pepperdine University. My area of emphasis was specifically within alternative dispute resolution (ADR) and was 100 percent focused on identifying and resolving conflict. After decades of wading through what I believed to be some of the most contentious situations imaginable, it didn't seem a stretch for me to already consider myself somewhat of an expert in this field. Truthfully, at the time, I felt I needed a break from healthcare, and law school provided a wonderful opportunity for me to deepen my understanding of conflict resolution.

Then, out of nowhere, just before I began my law program at Pepperdine, Julianne Williams—a great friend and mentor who was instrumental in helping to launch my career in healthcare and to whom I owe a great deal professionally—asked if I would assist her with a healthcare operation she owned and operated. It had 217 beds and all sorts of challenging complexities. She wanted to work with me in particular because we'd partnered together at this same building in the 1990s. This opportunity presented a chance for us to reconnect and resurrect our work together from the past. So, twenty-three years after working with Julianne, we teamed up again in the fall of 2019.

As 2019 drew to a close, little did we know what COVID had in store—or that it even existed. A few months later, in March 2020, the cases started coming in. At the time, attorneys were getting involved and immediately threatening to sue if there was one death at a nursing home. Of course, they didn't know how transmissible it was or how quickly it would spread throughout the country. Everyone was scared and in the dark.

It was also an emotional time for me personally, because my aunt had Alzheimer's and was actually a patient at our facility. COVID drastically changed every process typically involved with operating a nursing home. From the way that family members were suddenly not allowed onto the premises to the intrusive manner in which we had to check employees into their shifts, it was clear that our world would never be the same again. These life-altering adjustments also extended into my home life as well. As just one of many examples, when I would arrive home at the end of each day, in order for me to interact with my family, I had to take off my clothes in the garage, throw a towel around my waist, and head straight to the shower before even a hint at normal family interactions.

The skilled nursing facility was the largest in the region, and we had more COVID patients than most other nursing homes within the community. Once the pandemic hit everywhere else, the impact was profound. I walked through our quarantine areas in a hazmat suit. The whole situation felt surreal.

In a strange way, I felt grateful to Julianne for asking me to do the impossible; to somehow navigate the continuously evolving COVID protocols and regulations in California, to somehow keep patients safe and healthy during a once-in-a-century pandemic. When I took the position, I'd envisioned settling in for a nice, relatively calm and relaxing year, but instead the world changed in completely unforeseen ways—and the experience changed me. I thought I had conflict all figured out, but clearly I had more to learn.

Close to thirty patients died at the facility during the spring and early summer of 2020. As a percentage of our total population, that wasn't the worst outbreak experienced in our area by a long shot. However, as an absolute number, it was staggering and painful. It would be a long time before we had a clearer picture of COVID.

Then, one of our employees, a lovely and amazing woman who was one of the most dedicated people I've ever had the privilege of working with, got sick. I didn't realize how poorly she was doing until she started texting me from the hospital. At first, she texted, "I'm okay. I just have a cough." A couple of days later, she said the doctors were talking about a ventilator, but this employee still thought everything would be okay. She was incredibly dedicated, and even during this health crisis—while laid up in the hospital—she didn't want to let me down. Believe it or not, she'd actually planned to get some work done remotely in her condition. As each day progressed, she updated me via text about her condition and how challenging it was all becoming. Then, I was startled one morning to receive a text from her stating that she was having trouble breathing. I couldn't believe how quickly her health was declining. I was equally shocked that even in her darkest hour, she still conveyed hope and a spark of optimism. I'll never forget the last text I received from her: "I don't know how much more of this I can take." The next day, I got a call to say she'd passed. I cried my eyes out when I received that call. To this day, I've never erased those texts.

I'd been looking at our patients through the lens of their age, acuity levels, and comorbidities, assuming these factors alone dictated the course of their illness, but this employee's experience showed me the full gravity of the situation. Anyone could get COVID, and yes, in certain cases, it could be fatal. Until that point, I had a purely intellectual understanding of how to address conflict, but I hadn't fully lived it in a life-or-death situation. COVID changed that.

Conflict isn't always directly person-to-person. Sometimes, we think we've got everything figured out, and then life thrusts us into chaos. Think about it: What are the different ways conflict has shown up in your life? It's not always a relational problem with an individual. Often, the dynamic isn't so black and white.

There are components of the UNITY process that help when facing external conflict. It's a toolkit with broad applications, regardless of your career or circumstances. It won't instantly solve every conflict, but it helps build the muscle of addressing adversity. If anything in life is guaranteed, it's that we'll keep facing new and different challenges for as long as we inhabit this planet we call Earth.

What's Next?

You now have a deeper understanding of the roots of conflict and a heightened awareness that those origins run deep. We can see that conflict is the true underlying source of so many struggles—hiring challenges, poor employee retention, culture deficits, costly litigation, a lack of growth and innovation . . . the list goes on. It even touches on what can be a manifestation of your own internal conflict: Both the fear of success and the inability to achieve the triumphs you've always sought can be traced back to some element of personal or organizational conflict.

The answer, if you ask me, is UNITY. And now that we have a better understanding of how we arrived at this point, we turn our gaze to what lies ahead.

CHAPTER 2

UNITY Conflict Resolution: Before We Begin

Because I'm a firm believer that the "why" behind our beliefs and actions matters, before we dive into exactly what UNITY is, how it works, and why it gets results, let me take you back to 2019, when the seeds of UNITY were planted.

After having been in the healthcare industry for nearly the entirety of my career, I suddenly found myself on the outside looking in. It was not of my own choosing, and that was the most painful part. I was at a crossroads—one compounded by the fact that my departure wasn't quite the way I wanted to leave an industry I'd long loved. In those complex days that followed, I felt shame that the exit was not what I'd had in mind. There was both a sour taste in my mouth and also a hint of nostalgia—two symptoms, in this case, of an unresolved sense of calling.

The circumstances led me to reflect on the arc of my career and all the people I worked with. As I searched and tried to figure out my next calling, I asked myself, *What went right, and what could've gone better?*

The catalyst for my departure, as you might have guessed, had been a series of conflicts.

Part of me was relieved to move on, but I also experienced every emotion you can imagine. Throughout my life, I'd always felt I could control any situation I encountered, but this experience proved me wrong. It represented a loss of control.

Creating the conflict resolution framework UNITY offered a productive home for my energy and a practical vehicle for all the lessons I'd learned about conflict along the way. In short, it felt like a way to regain control of my life.

The framework didn't come together overnight, but the transition out of my business led me to start reflecting. I wrote a business plan and thought about all the attorneys, mediators, and arbitrators I'd worked with on court cases, which had obvious conflicts, as well as other relationships I'd had with less obvious points of contention. *What made some relationships great and others hard?* I wondered. *What was my role—how could I have made them better?*

After being so passionate about healthcare for so long, this self-reflection helped me be honest with myself and consider my next move. Before I began my next journey, I decided that I needed to be very intentional and thoughtful about my landing spot. I knew I had to meet the moment in a way that ventured beyond what I'd spent decades already doing. Though I knew I couldn't ignore all of my meaningful career experiences, I felt compelled to build upon them in new ways. Then, early one morning, it occurred to me that my situation required a total and complete reboot.

It hit me deeply and profoundly that healthcare operations weren't the only muscles I'd been building over the years. I'd spent decades traversing employee and organizational minefields and could utilize the many tools I'd developed throughout my career. Conflict resolution was where I needed to be. But first, I needed to pursue more education in the field of law and mediation to help people resolve conflicts in lasting and profound ways. I had work left undone, and I felt called to make other people's lives conflict-free, and to do so immediately.

When I think back on that time, I see I had all the puzzle pieces of UNITY, but I hadn't yet put them together. Once I took inventory of the concepts and synthesized them, UNITY was born. At Fusion, the company I'd go on to found around UNITY, I adopted a scientific mindset, formulating a hypothesis and then working through the different combinations of ideas in a systematic way, observing the results. That trial and error helped me discover what worked and what didn't, leading me to see ways I could have improved some of the toxic relationships in my own past.

Of course, I thought about the inauspicious start to my career using Dick's playbook and the time I modeled unhealthy and somewhat tyrannical behavior. I could have spent so much more time learning how to be the purposeful and genuine in my leadership skills and the ways in which I approached my staff and others. Those negative experiences led to a heightened self-awareness. My early clients undoubtedly saw us working out the steps in real time, and it definitely wasn't perfect. But, in the end, the many pieces of one of the most complicated puzzles of my lifetime FINALLY began to come together, and when it did . . . I never looked back.

Those steps eventually became a conflict management framework that has been studied in-depth and put into practice by scores of companies and leaders to address thousands of conflicts involving countless individuals. UNITY is succeeding in substantial and impactful ways across a multitude of platforms and organizations—a true full circle moment.

UNITY: The Bigger Picture

UNITY is a framework for conflict resolution. It's different from other foundational dispute approaches in this space because most solutions tend to be one sided and hyperfocused on speed: *How quickly can you reach a resolution?* Those quick-hit remedies often lack not only intention and reflection, but also staying power. You may hear some people say, "Stand your ground. The other person will respect that." By contrast, I'm more interested in encouraging people to to be initiators rather than procrastinators. By somehow feeling "stronger" when you hold your ground and wait for the other party to make the first move, you are only stunting whatever potential success you could've hoped to achieve. You are also undermining the potential for one of the most profoundly impactful lessons you will ever discover on planet Earth: the absolute freedom that only comes when you finally decide to act instead of being acted upon when conflict begins to permeate multiple areas of your life. UNITY is the portal to show you how.

UNITY is a structured approach in which each of the steps interconnect. They coexist within an ecosystem and work together when the steps are followed correctly.

The self-driven nature of the process allows you to achieve meaningful transformation within yourself regardless of the other party's initial investment. After completing the process, you not only have the tools to resolve the problems at hand in an effective way, but you also build the muscle to address future conflicts that will undoubtedly arise.

In addition, because the process avoids judgment, scorn, and threats, you can look at your thought processes with clarity and honesty, extending a soft invitation to others and leading by example. If you're willing to first look in the mirror and take an inventory of your own areas for growth, then inviting another person to do the same doesn't feel accusatory. Instead of starting with the immediate problem, the UNITY framework goes directly to work on the origin and source of the conflict. In turn, UNITY develops people into preeminent problem solvers, equipped to tackle the most complex disagreements within any organization or family.

UNITY brings individuals and groups together in a way that can forever change your bond and abilities not just to work together and coexist but also to become united in purpose. I believe that by the end of UNITY, you'll feel a deep sense of connection with those who you've previously been in conflict with and will also achieve something even greater: You've done more than fix a problem. You've built a permanent and profound skillset that will serve you for a lifetime.

UNITY goes much deeper than simple conflict resolution. The process works for one-on-one disputes and can also be applied to team and family environments. In this chapter, we lay the groundwork. In the following chapters, you'll learn each step in sequential order and find practical application exercises to empower you to address the conflicts holding you back.

Given the power dynamics at play when using UNITY in a work setting, it's critical not to work outside of company policy and to be very intentional with the steps, ensuring proper communication occurs. In other words, follow what's appropriate for your work context. Don't do things that will be frowned upon in the setting. Also, don't hijack or catch people off guard if you can help it. Don't interrupt the flow of business. Find a time and place that's appropriate. UNITY isn't a get-out-of-jail-free card to confront someone and derail their core work, and cultural norms and company rules still apply.

Walking the Talk

Fifteen years before I created the UNITY process, I was living it.

When I returned to my roots of senior care management in late 2004, after having worked alongside my dad and brother for the prior three years, I took over as the licensed administrator of a 120-bed skilled nursing facility in Central California. I have to admit, I felt intimidated upon my return as I recognized that I was a bit rusty. Additionally, there was another nursing facility, under the same company banner, directly across the street. I quickly discovered through various interactions with my team that the other facility was considered the gold standard of all twenty-eight operations within the corporation. Their strong financial performance, regulatory compliance, and employee retention and recruitment benchmarks all screamed success.

When I first began this journey, my building had spent the last five years going through one administrator after another—due in large part to its inability to deal with external competitive factors as well as a perpetual state of heightened conflict with its sister operation directly across the street. Even though they both were part of the same company, they had a deep history of division and animus toward one another. Once I took over management of the building, it was clear which of the two operations usually came out on top, and here's a little hint: It was not the one where my office resided. Indeed, for many years, my predecessors had not only felt that they couldn't compete, but the results clearly pointed out that their assertions were correct. In literally all measurables used to determine clinical and financial success, the place I now considered my "home away from home" always seemed to lag far, far behind.

Generally, I see myself as very thoughtful and amiable when it comes to interpersonal relationships. I keep an even keel, but when it comes to performing in my job at the highest level possible, I can be quite competitive. When I started at this new building, that natural competitive instinct took over, and my inclination was to go full bore in competition with the administrator across the street. There is no other way to put it: I resented that I'd inherited an operation that was nowhere near where my new colleague had achieved. I'm not saying this attitude represented my "finest hour," but alas, this was the reality of where I found myself in the fall of 2004. As unpleasant as my professional demeanor was at the time, that was my certainty. That was my truth.

In 2005, after several months in my new role, I hadn't achieved anywhere near what the company expected. I found myself derailed and paralyzed by jealousy and hostility. Finally, I decided to view my murky and perilous situation through a different lens. In that moment, I made a decision to take a different course from all the other administrators who had come before me. It was clear that digging in and getting adversarial wouldn't work in the long run. I had to change my attitude. I did NOT want to look back, months or years from then, and realize that my disdain and jealousy was the cause of self-imposed, self-sabotaging operational mediocrity that held me and my team back.

So, I bit my tongue. There was so much I wanted to say about how much I believed the other administrator and team conducted themselves and their operation, but instead, I made an immediate effort to find common ground. First, I introduced myself (can you believe it took me so long?) and took my counterpart out to lunch. "Wow, this is unusual," he said, because no one had ever done that before. Each step I initiated laid the groundwork for an approach that was counterintuitive and hard at first, but those strides began to develop our professional and personal relationship.

Once we started finding common ground, the results were astounding. It led to what became a core principle of the UNITY process: I started to realize we could have a mutually beneficial reality instead of playing a zero-sum game in which one of us had to lose for the other to win.

Now, don't get me wrong. It wasn't easy! Sometimes, every instinct told me *compete, win, dominate* to succeed in the company, but I took a step back and did the opposite. We both ended up becoming incredibly successful, and after the first year working together with this new approach, my building became the most profitable, with the preeminent regulatory compliance surveys throughout the entire portfolio. Our two operations spent the next several years competing.

But at the same time, we became each other's cheerleaders. Employees from both buildings became allies with shared visions and purpose. This was absolutely crucial in us achieving what neither of us ever thought possible: collaboration among competitors.

I'd stripped myself of envy, resentment, and anger and recognized that the synergy of our two competitive spirits could lead to success neither of us imagined. That realization helped drive success metrics for both businesses that increased five-, ten-, fifteen-fold over the next few years.

As we move through our lives, our motivations for doing things that are outwardly good and validating aren't always pure. It's worth asking yourself periodically, *Why am I doing what I'm doing?* Even if you're achieving the results and validation you want in the form of hitting your numbers or maintaining the status quo, sometimes a situation needs to change—and you have the power to change it.

The Confidence to Step Up

Mastering a skill brings newfound confidence. You don't want to hide what you know—you feel excited to use it, knowing you have the ability to overcome challenges. As a result, you can become a trusted leader in your group or organization, someone who knows how to deal with conflict and keep the purpose moving forward.

If you don't develop these skills, then someone else will step forward to handle conflict, often without the requisite abilities to do so. The results, in many cases, can and will be disastrous.

Have you ever been in a class when the instructor asks a question, and you think you know the answer, but you're afraid to raise your hand because you believe your response will come across as naive or just plain dumb? You hold off, only for someone else to say the exact same thing you would have said? And to pour salt into the wound, the instructor and other classmates verbalize approval and appreciation for such an eloquent and intelligent response. You kick yourself, wondering, *Why didn't I speak up?*

I often think about those moments when we have the choice to step up or, conversely, hold back when conflict is present. The first time using UNITY, it will probably feel awkward and scary. However, if you see the process through to completion, I predict you'll be glad you spoke up. That success builds confidence. The process has power individually, and you can magnify that impact through collective cultural change. I've seen people go from regretting that they didn't speak up to actively advocating for greater understanding without an ounce of remorse.

UNITY allows you to show up authentically and put your best foot forward in a way that's compassionate and kind. It has the potential to achieve amazing outcomes, but at the end of the day, the external payoffs are secondary to the profound internal shift.

The Headwind vs. Tailwind Paradox

Sometimes in business or in life, we assume that when we have a tailwind, everything we add to the direction we're heading will be good. However, I'd argue it's extremely beneficial when you have a headwind and things are working against you in a variety of settings and circumstances. In my experience, the people most motivated to implement the UNITY process are those who often face headwinds. When things aren't going as well, they dig even deeper, recognize the obstacles, try implementing fresh ideas, and look to develop positive outcomes. Difficulties and adversity can serve as just the invitation we need in the moment when it's required most and will act as a catalyst for necessary and permanent changes.

People with tailwinds may start to expect success without effort and ingenuity. Successful practitioners of the UNITY framework, on the other hand, don't take anything for granted. It's self-starting: One person recognizes conflict and adversity, leading them to say, "I'm going to be the one to rise above all of this." They recognize that what they've been doing is not working. Headwinds, as unpleasant as they may be, actually offer the perfect opportunity to do something different.

If you're not aware, a tailwind could be propelling you in the wrong direction. When things are going well and the wind is at your back, you may continue to do what you've been doing, whether or not it serves your relationship or organization in the long run. It's important to reassess whether it's time to try something different or dig deeper, because after all, tailwinds don't last forever.

Approached in the right spirit, it's an advantage to have more headwinds in business, because they force solutions you otherwise wouldn't know existed.

If you're reading this book, I'm guessing you're facing or expecting to face more headwinds. They're natural forces, and they inevitably return. Even if the going is easy right now, it's worth fortifying yourself with strategies for the next time conditions become more treacherous.

UNITY for Teams

Often, my team will work with individuals and groups, both large and small. As we engage and coach in these environments, we often encounter fractured and broken systems for communication, accountability, and any sense of buy-in to their company's vision and culture. In these surroundings, though we ultimately take our cues from executive leadership, our recommendation to the CEO is that we pull the entire team together initially, rather than just leaders of the organization. This is to avoid skewed and biased perceptions from the top brass from the jump. It is always beneficial to receive unfiltered and candid responses from those in the trenches.

It's so rewarding to work with leaders who understand this principle of how unfettered access to entire teams increases the chance for long-term viability and success of key initiatives within the organization.

Once, I provided an action plan to an owner whose company was on the brink of collapse. We pulled the entire team together, including people in active conflict. We both agreed that ripping the Band-Aid off, rather than gingerly meeting with individual groups, was critical and necessary for *real* results to be achieved.

We put up large sheets of paper on walls all around the conference room, with a different question written down on each individual page. Each sheet had titles like *communication fixes, collaboration boosters, trust-building ideas,* and *what they wished others knew.* Everyone was looking awkwardly at each other and scanning the room, trying to figure out what was happening and exactly when this exercise would end.

Before turning people loose to answer, we laid some important groundwork. "This is a unique environment," I told them. "I've been given permission from the head of the company to have this conversation. Instead of talking confidentially in small groups, he wants us to acknowledge what's really going on without sugarcoating anything. No one is wrong to have strong opinions." I didn't reveal the extent of my knowledge of the particular issues. Instead, I had them tell me. Then, we broke down the fundamental challenges leading to cultural toxicity within their organization. At first, the conversation turned very accusatory, with people literally pointing fingers at one another.

While they talked and occasionally yelled and screamed, I took notes under the appropriate headings on the large sheets of paper so that we had a common understanding of the issues and people felt heard and validated. I said each time, as I wrote down their responses,

"I completely understand why that's so frustrating." We went through every single response. The owner acknowledged he was part of the problem, and he knew people would say some uncomfortable things about him and his approaches. It was a more structured and much more comprehensive and documented version of the intervention my staff had with me early in my career.

At the end of the day, this experience was the most head-on, aggressive approach I'd been a part of with an organization. It was also one of the best meetings we ever had.

It didn't devolve into total chaos and even more damaging disagreements because people followed what we were there to accomplish. We acknowledged every contribution, no matter how "out there" it sounded. We wrote down absolutely every comment offered by the employees and validated their truths, rather than picking, choosing, and contradicting.

That's a hugely important part of facilitating team cohesion that we've discovered when working directly with employees: Validate with zero judgment and allow them to express any and all thoughts without interruption. And, without a doubt, the most important skill that we've developed over time and that we preach from the rooftops to our clients is summed up simply with the acronym LRRA (**L**isten intently, **R**esist the urge to interrupt, **R**estate their positions in order to validate mutual understanding, and **A**cknowledge you understand their positions, no matter how vastly different they may be from your own).

I received some extremely valuable feedback after that training, and not just from the owner and head of HR. Surprisingly, even many whom were identified by ownership as the "ring leaders" of the decline of their workplace culture pulled me aside after our work together. They were ecstatic at not only having the opportunity to air their feelings and believing they were actually heard, but having hope for the first time that their own leadership would be initiating this important principle forevermore.

The foundation of this work in a group setting is getting everyone together and on the same page, as uncomfortable as that may be. As experienced as I am with this model, that meeting taught me new things I hadn't yet discovered:

- Sometimes the best and most productive meetings are the most uncomfortable ones.
- When we really want to know what other people think of us at work, it's best to pull them together and ask them directly.
- Owners, managers, and executives who desire real and lasting change are willing to have every voice heard and accept others' truths rather than exclusively relying on their own preconceived notions.
- Successful organizations communicate fiercely, and they don't punish people for speaking their truths.

The experience with this company presented a fair number of challenges, some of which we'd attacked for the very first time working with and coaching teams. Due to the many complexities and variables with this group and their deep-seated challenges, it became necessary to coordinate follow-up sessions to that hugely successful initial meeting. We returned and broke into smaller groups for targeted UNITY training, focusing on how these particular employees could be the ones to initiate the process and not assume someone else would eventually step in.

In small-group sessions, I encouraged people to brainstorm unresolved conflicts that were sapping their energy and attention—whether the relationship was at work, in their family, at church, or elsewhere. I didn't suggest digging up old grudges but rather learning to meet ongoing issues head-on. Once they identified those top three to five conflicts and were trained in the steps, the goal was for them to feel empowered enough to start initiating resolution. By the time everyone had received this training, it transformed the ecosystem of their entire company. Instead of the status quo, which included disrespect toward colleagues and fractured interdepartmental communication, we witnessed a complete cultural overhaul. Instead of the usual undermining and subversive behavior, we watched right before our eyes as, one by one, these employees took satisfaction and great pride in building up individuals and teams through words—and not just through words, but through the direct and impactful actions of outward respect all across the operation. What a sight to behold!

Best Practices for Implementation

Before we move into exploring each step, here are a few interrelated best practices for implementing UNITY that will set you up for success.

Be Willing to Acknowledge Your Role

Problems in an organization ultimately come back to individual relationships. You have a role in the dynamic of your whole organization, whether immediately apparent to you or not. It might be tempting to ask, *How is the employee retention problem my fault?* Or, *What does the conflict between those two cubicle mates over there have to do with me?* It's easy to justify staying at arm's length, but the core of an organization is always personal relationships. Stronger personal relationships mean stronger organizations. And stronger organizations mean the potential for success at every single level.

It's true that manager-report relationships are different from friendships. However, we can still promote strong connections at work. If we are not spending as much time investing in our work relationships as we are with processes and improvement within the organization, we will never achieve the desired results.

So, yes, maintain healthy boundaries, but it's okay—and beneficial—to cultivate a sense of comradery and commonality. Having a positive relationship at work doesn't mean becoming too close. It simply means discovering what makes people unique and what bonds them together.

For years, I've worked with a highly talented individual named Nicole. She excelled in areas of personnel management, team building, and as director of marketing within various healthcare operations and settings. Specifically within that latter role, there was a reason success seemed to always follow her efforts: Nicole simply talked to people in natural and genuine ways, got to know them on personal rather than purely "business" levels, and had a knack for remembering everything they shared with her about their lives. Nicole never gave slick sales presentations or tried to strong-arm people into touring our nursing facilities or other operations. She spent 100 percent of her time focused on organically bonding with people. Not for show, not for profits, but because that's who Nicole is, and that's always what she's been about. And as a result, the sales always seemed to follow.

Everyone else in her role that I worked with over the years seemed to engage in what I referred to as "feature vomiting." Simply put, they'd start listing all the reasons they were better than the competition, but in the end, more often than not, they simply made themselves sound like the competition.

Getting to know people on a very deep level does not take one iota away from your productivity—in fact, it enhances your ability to get things done. You don't need to go to happy hour with your team after work, but if you spend a third of your life with them, doesn't it make sense to invest in and care about them, their priorities, and their families?

Businesses are made of people. If you strengthen your teams through finding commonality and mutual investment, individuals will want to do their best for other members of their team and avoid disappointing each other. Building relationships the right way leads to an extremely productive—and much more enjoyable—symbiosis.

When you get to know people well, you naturally start to see points of connection where they can help you and vice versa, both inside and outside the organization. In that state, teamwork and sales flow naturally. You make decisions that drive the business without it feeling coldly transactional. Nicole is that rare individual who does an incredible job of focusing on individual relationships and connecting in real and profound ways. Whatever success follows for Nicole has, and always will be, secondary to the meaningful relationships she makes with countless individuals she has come in contact with over decades.

My amazing wife, Kathryn, has a similar ability to connect with people, make them feel great about themselves, and then keep the bigger picture in mind. She's not banking points for her advantage. She genuinely cares about others and is highly organized in remembering and documenting details of their lives. If someone mentions the anniversary of a death, she remembers it years later and continues to acknowledge that difficult anniversary in their lives. Kathryn is just as effective at recalling other important dates and milestones, such as birthdates of her friends' new babies, high school and college graduations of friends' kids and grandkids, and important career and promotion milestones. She immediately acknowledges these important life events with thoughtful notes and other affirmations. Doing so makes people feel seen. She has no ulterior motive; Kathryn just wants to show people she cares.

Relationships are not about just being nice to other people; they deepen when you treat people like they sincerely matter to you and when you remember things that are meaningful to them. Why do we invest in others? Because it's the right thing to do. And there is also another major benefit that is not talked about enough; giving our sincere time and attention to others also makes a major impact in reducing and ultimately resolving disputes and disagreements.

Move Past Blame

You may be wondering how to initiate the UNITY process without sounding like you're blaming others. Going through this process simply requires the willingness to ask, *What's my role in this?* We often talk about what *not* to say when you first approach someone you're in conflict with. Specifically, we challenge people not to use the word "you." To ensure the other party doesn't feel blamed, talk about your own role within the disagreement.

You might say, "We have worked together for a long time. I have recognized that we are doing really well in so many areas, but it's clear that there are some opportunities for me to improve. I know that when we work together, we are capable of achieving anything!"

It may sound like you're avoiding the obvious, but there's plenty of time to get to the heart of the issue. The initial steps are about self-reflection. Once you identify your role and take ownership, you know what your part in the process is. So, when you do approach the other person, there's not the temptation to blame. You may have initially thought the majority of the conflict was their fault, but doing the preparatory work will show each party the part they play and the piece of the conflict they own and you own.

Let me make it crystal clear . . . it's not that you're blaming yourself for everything. You're just focusing on the parts you have direct control over, to avoid driving the other person so far away that there will be little chance for success in the future.

Once you make a list of what you see as the points of disagreement, you can share it with the person with whom you're in conflict with. You might say, "Initially, I thought our positions were vastly different, but once I did a little homework thinking through our situation, I realized we have so much more in common than I originally thought." At this point, you might still have deep disagreement with the other party's conduct or position on an issue, but you're finding a common meeting place. It's not your job to take responsibility for everything that has transpired up to this point. Your only assignment in this early stage is to be at a place in which you can simply and factually articulate what your role was within this conflict.

I find it most effective to approach this situation in a lighthearted way, saying something to them like, "Can you believe I did homework on what I can do better? But it was super instructive, because I realized I didn't understand your perspective." Taking the time to communicate that level of investment and care will naturally invite the other person to soften their stance. Remember that it's a conversation, not an accusation.

Be Open

This may sound counterintuitive, but when doing this valuable work to improve yourself, include others within the organization. It's so important for disparate parties to be involved, provide support, and have buy-in as you invite them in. In my experience, when you operate in a vacuum, there's not the necessary support to ensure that the desired changes are permanent and sustainable.

The most successful outcomes with conflict resolution are not hiding in the shadows with minimal involvement. The best processes surface many points of view and raise awareness of what's happening at all levels. It takes some experience and time to be vulnerable enough to look within and consider your role in resolving conflict between people or teams. It also takes skill not only to accept criticism but also to acknowledge the truth in it and then identify the first step you're responsible for. Openness, transparency, and involving as many different viewpoints as possible will lead to the best possible outcomes.

Often the person with whom you are at odds with still has ill will toward you, even as you move forward in the process. In those cases, it's good to get other perspectives from people who don't have a dog in the fight. Especially in the early stages, they can often see situations more clearly and directly. You may also be more open to hearing feedback from a neutral party rather than someone in conflict with you.

Perhaps like many of you, my natural state has always been not to share my baggage with others. But to transform relationships for the better, we have to get out of our own way and begin to see our flaws with keenly sharper vision.

Though this is hard to admit, I believe there's value in revisiting painful lessons from our past. There was a time many years ago in which my impulse was to avoid admitting my flaws, and if I was entrenched in an active conflict, I attempted to handle it in secret. Plenty of executives would still say that's the best approach to avoid having issues spill over within their organizations. However, the value of obtaining more input by reexamining past mistakes and missteps isn't for people to choose sides and get pulled into the conflict. It's to gain helpful perspective that allows both parties to move toward a resolution.

It's also hard to admit when you have an issue if you're the one whom the buck stops with. There's pressure to project confidence that everything is fine and to signal you're winning and achieving. Admitting you're struggling with something profound may feel like you're being knocked off whatever pedestal you've built up for yourself, but done well, it achieves much better results than trying to fix everything behind the scenes. When you harness more points of view on a particular issue, you can solve it in a way that is faster, more thorough, and sustainable, turbocharging your future work.

Practice Self-Awareness and Get Buy-In

Effective businesses requires maturity. You don't have to be a leader to be in conflict. However, if you are in a management role, you have more latitude about who you pull in for perspective. If you're frontline staff, it takes more courage to approach those in authority to seek solutions. But when done thoughtfully, it can create a powerful connection with those who are often in the best position to affect positive change in an otherwise difficult situation.

One of my favorite things is being in a position to help people come up with conversational strategies for approaching management, such as saying, "Look, it's no secret that Sally and I have been struggling on this issue, and if you didn't know that, I'm just keeping you in the loop. I want you to know I'm very self-aware of the situation and trying to solve it. I'd love your input about how to proceed." Though it might feel uncomfortable at first, getting early buy-in from your supervisor or mentor is a good idea. I can't think of any manager worth their salt who would dismiss a sincere attempt to get the team working together better. So whether you're on the front lines or a senior leader, communicate with others who can help you in the process. Doing so helps create the necessary foundation to facilitate anchored and long-term sustainability.

Prioritize Clarity, Not Alliances

When deciding who to talk to, approach it in the spirit of resolving the situation, not picking someone who will tell you that you're "right" all the time. If you have a conflict with a family member, it might feel good to find another member of your household who will side with you, but that only stokes the fire. The goal is to gain clarity so that everyone wins, not collect backup so that you can claim victory. In the case of a family conflict, you might say, "Your sister and I have had issues, and I just want to let you know I'm going to reach out. She doesn't have to see things from my point of view, but here's how I'm feeling. And if you have anything that would help me understand her better, that would be so helpful."

That's a conversation in the spirit of openness rather than trying to marshal alliances. Alliances might work when you're competing on *Survivor*, but ganging up is never good in real life. Most of the time we want people to be on our side because it makes us feel empowered. The irony is it's actually much more empowering to truly understand what motivates others, rather than having them hanging on your every word. That kind of power is solid and real, unlike the brittle, easily lost power of getting people to agree with us to feed our own inflated sense of self. When we do the work in attempting to see others' perspectives, we actually gain the kind of strength that invites trust, honesty, and integrity from those whom we may be in conflict with.

Particularly if you're in a position of authority, getting people to agree with you will only serve to your blind spots. They may validate poorly constructed opinions because they're afraid of repercussions. Without truth and clarity, organizations are hamstrung and will never reach their ultimate potential.

When I'm training and coaching teams about this very issue, I call it the "alliance fallacy"—the notion that you feel more power when there's conflict by seeking and latching onto alliances. In reality, you don't gain power; your allies have their own individual motivations and are often currying favor, which leads to a false sense of trust. It's transactional and further deepens the chasm between you and the person you're at odds with, because often you get caught up in psychological warfare instead of trying to understand and reach mutually beneficial solutions. When it comes to resolving disputes, alliances with outside parties only alienate us and drag out the conflict vastly longer than is necessary.

UNITY in Action: The Case Study of StrongSpring

Throughout the book, we'll return to a composite case study of a company I'll call StrongSpring to give you concrete examples of how UNITY applies to organizations and teams. While your specific situation will undoubtedly be different, there's so much we can learn by following an example and learning through the experiences and stories of others. As you read about StrongSpring, I bet you'll realize that in many ways, you're discovering truths about yourself too. That's the whole point!

StrongSpring: The Basics

Marley is a business owner who began her venture, StrongSpring, nine and a half years ago. It took off and experienced tremendous growth in a short period of time, now with about seven hundred employees. However, in recent years, when compared to their successful launch nearly a decade ago, they find themselves backsliding and losing market share at a critical juncture in their short history. Generally speaking, they are underachieving or just barely hitting their financial targets and have been chronically average when compared to their prior year-over-year financial outcomes. In other words, even from the outside of this privately held company, it's painfully obvious that StrongSpring seems to lack the clear direction it once had. And as if all of that wasn't bad enough, top leadership in the company is suffering from a case of "we don't know what we don't know" syndrome. Clearly Marley and her management team know there are issues driving the downturn, but they haven't yet articulated how best to define those obstacles and what the first steps are in doing a reset with StrongSpring's course.

StrongSpring enjoyed early, exponential customer growth, but that strong trajectory is slowing because their once-proud company culture has declined to a state of outright toxicity. One of the biggest factors in this downturn has been the inability of StrongSpring's home office to anticipate what their field operations need and for the employees within field operations to properly communicate their own specific wants and wishes. Some key mid-level managers in the field blame the home office, saying that field workers aren't supported adequately, that the home office is incompetent, and that they could "run the company" better themselves.

Complicating matters is the fact that StrongSpring's systems and policies have not evolved at all. The workforce is not on track for a "light bulb moment" any time soon—no one has decided they need to do things any differently. So, in the current state, the organization operates in an uninspiring way. Upsetting the applecart could provide great results, but people are too fearful that change would have the opposite effect, causing them to backslide. They're afraid to take risks.

Culturally, leadership rarely, if ever, organizes retreats or plans morale-building activities or events. The mood feels much like the birthday party for the boss, Bill Lumbergh, in the 1999 film *Office Space* when all the cake gets passed around and there's none left for Milton. Everyone sings "Happy Birthday," but it's monotone—there's no passion. It's all about the *TPS reports* . . . IYKYK! The relationship of subordinate to executive is very defined, and the leaders at StrongSpring want it that way. It gives them a feeling of self-importance.

In underperforming companies where the executives lack vision and creativity, they generally latch on to something of little consequence or value to make them feel successful. That very strong subordinate-to-boss relationship is their drug, when in reality, performance would be so much greater if the leaders focused on exceeding expectations, motivating people, and developing new and more effective ways to do business.

A true leader knows they have some influence in supporting workers, and they celebrate and express pride in the people who get the job done. At StrongSpring, though, that's not what's transpiring. Most employees don't feel celebrated. They know their place, and they simply clock in and out each day. With the overemphasis on hierarchy and the lack of fresh vision, there's a sense of stagnation and frustration. There's a huge gap between how the organization is currently performing and the potential for what it could be. Unlike when they first launched and in every way possible exuded energy, excitement, and enthusiasm, StrongSpring has migrated to a place where they are content to experience a modicum of success instead of reaching for their greatest possible potential.

Overall, the company is coasting for now, and everything seems fine on the surface—but underneath lie the seeds of conflict that people aren't yet aware of. Leadership is much less concerned with what drives and motivates people than with policies, procedures, and position titles. As a result, they're achieving the basics, the bare minimum, the average.

In those scenarios, occasionally something dramatic or catastrophic happens, but in general, conflict tends to be a very slow build. The message to line staff is to maintain the status quo, so most tend to give barely enough of themselves to get by.

Apathy and stagnation trickle down from highest levels of the company and permeate throughout StrongSpring. Leaders model that they aren't striving, setting the expectation that no one else will either. In the moments when they make a gesture toward team building, as when singing "Happy Birthday," it feels like a sham. It doesn't mean that conflict's not present; it just doesn't tend to manifest in a visible way.

There's a saying that the opposite of love isn't hate—it's indifference. Risking productive conflict is an act of love, and as we move forward with StrongSpring, we're going to discover how.

StrongSpring: The Roller Coaster

Sometimes we work with companies like StrongSpring, whose results are always on a perpetual "roller coaster." Their performance is very uneven, like the most volatile stock market. Someone will get super energized to create change and apply a fair amount of effort to make something happen, but it's not sustainable because leadership isn't fully bought in.

There's personal investment for a higher, better purpose among certain levels of leadership, but it's inconsistent. The organization isn't fully aligned or willing to take the necessary risks, so there's an unproductive push-and-pull dynamic. If only part of the organization is invested, or if everyone understands the value of changing in theory but won't put it into practice, poor results will follow.

When line-staff employees sense that upper management is disingenuous in its purpose and mission, their behavior follows suit. If improvement is just a matter of lip service, then everyone will be half in, half out, dipping their toe in the pool but not jumping in. With inconsistent buy-in, there may be more visible conflict than at a company like StrongSpring. There are factions and blame, but it's not 100 percent toxic; there are periods when change gets underway, even though it later peters out again. The environment is confusing for employees: One month the financial metrics seem great and leaders act positive, but the next month they're disappointed and pointing fingers. The direction and expectations feel confusing and murky.

Whether there's visible or unseen conflict in your own personal situation, the importance of UNITY is based in the reality that it provides the tools that can transform individuals within organizations and positively impact families in meaningful and substantial ways. We speak to people who are passionate about what they're doing and willing to make a change. The good news is they can; the difficulty is that you will occasionally butt heads in order to do so. Though this is not always fun, it at least shows that both sides are invested, and there's a way forward.

What's Next?

Now that you're empowered with a deeper understanding of conflict as a whole and how the UNITY process works in the big picture—along with some best practices to ensure you're set up for success—it's high time we go to work exploring each part of the framework individually, starting with *unpack*.

CHAPTER 3

STEP 1: <u>U</u>npack

J uly 16, 2021.

"Oh my gosh, Dad," my son Will said through the FaceTime call. "I can't believe you made it!"

I was standing at the top of Mount Whitney, the tallest peak in the contiguous United States, fighting back tears as I looked at Will's face, somehow showing crystal-clear on the screen of my iPhone, 14,505 feet above sea level. And before you ask, no . . . I don't blame him for his pleasant surprise that I'd actually made it! It had been an extremely strenuous excursion, which he knew very well because he'd been in that exact same spot when he summited Mount Whitney five years earlier, in 2016, after a seventy-mile backpacking trip.

There's a backstory, of course: I love hiking, and a couple of very good friends of mine—Dave Garrett and Clint Brown—and I had taken quite a few hikes together with our sons and other young men in the ward's scouting program in the past. In the process, we'd become great friends, and in 2016, we started talking about the possibility of doing a trip on a grander scale. We had the idea that a group of us should do a seventy-mile backpacking trip. We'd begin in California's

Sequoia National Park and follow what's known as the Mineral King to Mount Whitney Route. As we began to discuss details in depth, I got more and more excited about our upcoming adventure. We would start the five-day hike at the Franklin Lakes Trailhead. We then would cross Franklin Pass, head through the Big Arroyo and Kern River drainages, join the John Muir Trail (JMT), and continue hiking north on the JMT up to Guitar Lake. Then, we'd ascend via the Mount Whitney Trail switchbacks all the way to the summit.

I was all in! However, much to my great dismay, I was called out of town for a work emergency the very week that this epic 2016 adventure was planned. Despite my best efforts, I simply could not find a way out of this conflict. I was devastated! I felt anger, resentment, and guilt over missing a trip that was at the top of my bucket list. To me, climbing a physical mountain is akin to the challenge of learning and growing from resolving a conflict. There are so many obstacles to overcome. I'd wanted to go even more because Will would be a part of this thrilling excursion, and I knew what an incredibly special shared experience that would have been for us.

I thought about him and the group on the day they were going to be summiting, and I had FOMO in the worst way. Then, I received the unexpected and tender mercy of my son calling me from the very top of Mount Whitney as they summited. There's no signal during the entirety of the wilderness hike, but a surprisingly strong one at the top of the mountain. When I answered, he said, "Dad, I made it!" He was so proud! I was so proud of him, too, that in the moment, all of my self-pity completely washed away. I'd felt so heavy carrying around those negative emotions, and such a gesture lightened my load, allowing me to get out of my own way and simply feel happy for him.

For the next several years, though, I still felt like something was missing—I wanted to summit the mountain and have that group experience too. So when Clint floated the idea of summiting a second time, I thought it sounded amazing. I'd been thrown a lifeline for a second chance at accomplishing something I had missed out on years earlier. He invited a few other friends from out of state to join us, and we ventured out very early on a July morning. Before I say anything else about our adventure, I must admit that it was the hardest hike of my life, bar none. I had good hiking boots, but I still found a way to blister both feet mercilessly. To make matters worse, I could never seem to find a way to fully hydrate during the five-day summit. I had plenty of water, but I failed to pack a sufficient amount of electrolytes and felt completely worn down from a fairly early stage of the hike, even though I'd thought that I had meticulously prepared for every last detail and every imaginable scenario. Plus, relatively speaking, I was also the "old man" of the group—eight years the senior than the next-oldest hiker.

Fortunately, despite the obvious challenges I faced, there was a bright spot as each day progressed and we would stop to eat our lunch and dinner. As we unpacked and ate each meal, we not only received energy and nutrients that we so desperately needed, our packs became a little lighter each time. Though gradual, this was crucial in easing our burdens just a bit and making an incredibly daunting climb a little less... well, daunting. Of course, on Mount Whitney, my bag was made lighter as each meal was consumed, but the mental and emotional toll lessened greatly as I accomplished something I'd missed out on those years earlier. The journey helped relieve my lingering guilt and made me feel more connected to Will. Walking the trail he and the rest of the group had walked, I viscerally understood their accomplishment and now was able to share in it. The process nourished me physically, mentally, and spiritually in deep and profound ways.

Never for an instant did I consider giving up. Clint is a pharmacist, and another friend who joined us, Ammon Rasmussen, is a general surgeon. Other people had blisters, too, but mine were much worse. When I took my shoes off, these men with medical training would

ask, "Are you sure you want to go on?" I insisted on continuing because I didn't want to miss out again. I would've crawled to the top
if I had to. By the way, considering my unexpected blistering fiasco
and the aid and assistance these two great men provided, they will
forever occupy a space on my own personal "Mount Rushmore" of
warriors who, in every way possible, lift, strengthen, and inspire all
within their sphere of influence.

We started early Monday morning and summited on Friday in
the early afternoon. It was five days, 69.5 miles, with a great deal of
altitude gain. On the last day, when we summited, I felt incredible
emotion. The trip had been so hard, yet I was beyond ecstatic. Despite
my elation, I felt a pang of sadness and wished my son could have been
there with me. Will was in Argentina, serving his two-year church
mission. On a whim, I decided if I had a signal, I'd try to FaceTime
him the way he'd called me from that same spot five years prior. I
knew it was a long shot to catch him since missionaries have such
tightly packed schedules—but lo and behold, he picked up. I screen-
shotted a moment from that conversation. Deep, unspoken emotions
passed between us. We shared something that we hadn't been able to
experience together all those years earlier. He knew exactly how I was
feeling because he'd been there too. And both of our "packs" were a
little lighter that day, having gone through such an experience—one
shared, albeit not in the traditional way.

My Mount Whitney experience, and the powerful analogy it
created in my mind and heart, has been a great reminder to me of
how UNITY brings people together in empathy and connection.
When one person wins in this model, we all win. We share in the
success, because there's enough to go around for all. And yes, when
we unpack all of those burdens that multiplied due to our inability
to make deep and abiding connections, our path becomes clearer and
our vision suddenly sharper.

And it all starts with *unpacking*.

Put It into Practice

Think back to a time when you were having a serious personal struggle with a friend, a member of your family, or a member of your team. When you were really at odds with that person and so sure that you were right, what did that feel like for you? Did you experience any empathy or compassion at the height of the conflict? Reflect on the situation and write down the problem, the stakeholders, and your initial emotions/approach.

Preparing to Unpack

In my experience it's fairly rare, at the very outset of a heated conflict, for two people to lean in with empathy and compassion. This resistance is normal! When we think we're right, we often dig in our heels.

Given that natural tendency, it can be challenging in work settings for the two parties to initially work out all of their issues when emotions are at their zenith. When we work with clients in group settings, we like to break the ice by doing some get-to-know-you exercises and building trust, sharing things like favorite movies and finding reasons for people to applaud each other. Then, without pressuring anyone, we ask for volunteers to share examples of a time when they were frustrated due to an argument, disagreement, or just not seeing eye to eye with someone. We invite them to share, in detail, the emotions they were experiencing, especially related to their feelings about the person they were in conflict with. As you can imagine, the response was often raw, bitter, and very revealing about the emotions they were feeling at the time. We make a point to purposely not to direct any attention to parties within these coaching clusters who we know are in active disputes. Though this exercise is anything but easy, it effectively sets the stage for how entrenched emotions, rather than issues, are intertwined into the very fabric of all conflicts.

Having laid that groundwork, we can move from reflecting on past personal conflicts to addressing existing organizational conflicts within the room.

Taking the First Step

The "U" in UNITY is about unpacking the biases you bring to a given conflict. We all have stories in our heads that influence how we approach others, and the goal is to take a clear look at those events in our lives. List seven to ten specific prejudices that you remain affixed to related to the conflict with the other party. Keep it simple and do not overcomplicate. And there is no need at this stage to add additional nuance or hidden meanings behind why your positions differ. The point of this exercise is just to record and differentiate your own positions relative to the biases that the other party brings to the table.

By listing why we think we're right, we can start to take an honest inventory. The stakes feel high in any conflict, and particularly in an organization where people are stuck in the status quo. It takes a brave soul to take the first step forward and confront the core issues that have planted their own toxic roots throughout an operation.

When we begin working with and coaching organizations that are mired in conflict, there is often a tendency by the employees to hold back or become cagey with what little information they choose to share. Additionally, as we guide and focus them through the *initial* stages of UNITY, it's rare that employees have the courage to initiate roleplays with their peers present, answer questions in group settings about how to resolve disputes, and are willing to be vulnerable by honestly describing their role in an organization's culture of conflict. However, by the time our UNITY coaching is complete, there is a palpable confidence that permeates and empowers even the most timid individuals.

In that first step in which you bare your own preconceived notions and personal prejudices, be brief and don't belabor the point. We'll get to digesting the other person's perspective a little later, but right now, it's just about surfacing your own beliefs, not challenging them.

When we kick off this exercise within groups, we start by asking about typical biases that each of us bring to our own personal dis- agreements with others. We articulate to the groups that by listing our own individual biases, we're honestly expressing that our perspectives are not always rational or accurate. Then, we start on the left side of the whiteboard, where we've recorded the group's responses to our prompts. As facilitators, we never edit or judge any of the responses provided by participants in this coaching.

The process validates that their own biases are not bad. The point is simply self-discovery of their position, not to make them feel wrong or terrible. Listing seven to ten biases is a good psychological exercise, because most people who haven't been through this process wouldn't even consider there could be so many reasons to be at odds with one another. Unexamined, conflict often simply carries a general sense of feeling wronged in some meaningful way. By digging deeply and stretching to find at least seven reasons, you start to get a fuller picture of the scenario and what's important to you about it.

This exercise is great in a workshop, but it's also something you can do on your own. We give participants homework to spend time in deep, personal reflection surrounding their own viewpoints that brought them to seek a new and clearer path.

> ### *Put It into Practice*
>
> *Take a notebook or digital device and list the seven to ten definitions or descriptions of your position on a pressing conflict. Why do you believe that you're correct in your assertions?*

Once you've pondered, internalized, and listed your own positions regarding the conflict at hand, this first step of UNITY then requires you to shift and consider what the other party's motivations and viewpoints related to this interpersonal clash may be. At this point in the *unpack* step, the goal is to identify and anchor where your differences truly lie.

I know it's hard because passions are high, but try to put yourself in the other person's position. Don't insert your own feelings or your belief system. Set your biases to the side. Temporarily sequester your deep-seated convictions with the idea that you will eventually revisit them, but not now. It's an exercise in taking perspective.

> ## Put It into Practice
>
> *Put yourself in the other person's shoes and ask the same question: Why do you think they think they are right in this instance? Don't worry about this being 100 percent accurate. Just do your best, based on what you imagine they would say.*

Start Internally

Developing these newfound perspectives on those issues that you assumed divided each of you helps to lay the essential groundwork prior to talking to the other person (That comes midway through the process, when we get to the "I" in UNITY.). First, though, we would benefit from a fair amount of self-discovery. Interacting face-to-face will crash and burn if you don't have these pieces in place. In this beginning phase, the other person doesn't have to know you're laying the groundwork for conflict resolution. The vast majority of the time, this process starts without two willing parties, just one brave individual who begins reflecting in a quiet moment.

Let's be honest: Sometimes it's hard to overcome our egos. However, it's worth it! If you're reading this book, you've tried the same thing one too many times and have probably even experienced some failures along the way. Now, you're finally ready to make a change.

When we first notice a conflict, it's natural to think the problem is with the other person and that we need to bring *them* in to work it out right away. A word of caution however; at this stage, I am advocating for you to pause and work through these steps in order, starting with *yourself.*

External conflict holds up a mirror for us. You don't know there's an issue internally with how you approach conflict until there's an external confrontation that forces that issue. That's why the first three steps of UNITY are all internal. There's an *interpersonal* manifestation, but the work begins *intrapersonally.* Through the lens of the external, we have the opportunity to engage in internal discovery and learn more about ourselves. If we've been in therapy, are unusually reflective and self-aware, or have noticed patterns in our previous interactions, maybe we've already been working on these issues to a certain extent, but interacting with others is where the moment of truth is revealed.

The key words in the acronym UNITY give a surface impression of what we need to do, but we need to dig deeper. At first glance, it may not be self-evident that *unpack, navigate,* and *identify common-alities* are all internally focused and driven, but they absolutely are. We don't immediately jump into collaboration with the other party; first, we need to lay the groundwork on our own.

If you've reached the point of picking up this book, you've probably tried other conflict resolution strategies that may not have worked. If you've previously moved straight to engaging with the other person, without laying critical groundwork to bring about the very best version of yourself, then it's time to finally try something different. Something lasting. Something permanent.

Common Pitfalls and Pushbacks When Unpacking

There are some familiar obstacles to this stage, which are worth considering in advance so that you can continue moving forward in the most effectual way possible. Sometimes people feel like the juice isn't worth the squeeze—it seems too painful to surface all the reasons the other person thinks they're right. Another is worrying that the other party won't be honest, so it seems unfair to be vulnerable and to open up if they won't do so as well.

From the outside, it might seem like the process involves an inordinate amount of effort with very little potential payback. That's a tempting interpretation at the beginning, when the other party still seems fully like an adversary. From that stance, it feels like there's no way they could meet you in the middle. I will say, in the early stages, you need to assume that your vision is still murky. It's through doing the work of seeing the person in another way that you gain clarity. They won't have done any of their own heavy lifting yet, but you can still take the emotion and personalization out of it.

There are also logistical concerns. It sounds clean and almost surgical when we're facilitating with a whiteboard, but how can individuals and teams roll out the process for real and incorporate it in their day-to-day routines? When we work with leaders who want to implement conflict resolution in their organizations, they often say their people don't have enough time to do the amount of reflection that we're asking of them. Or if they could theoretically make the time, they don't know that it's worth the investment. "What's the ROI?" is the question I most often get.

As individuals and organizations consider incorporating UNITY within their daily operating norms and routines, if they finally are in a place where getting serious about resolving their broken communication and toxic relationships is priority one, then maybe, just maybe, they'll have a shot at success. However, UNITY cannot be danced around, teased, or played with. It requires a fully entrenched commitment to be followed and committed to daily. If the approach to incorporating UNITY in any meaningful way is half hearted, it will never take root. But when planting the right seeds, in the most fertile soil, and when all other conditions are just right, UNITY can spring forth the most awe-inspiring, colorful relationships and culture that people and teams have ever experienced. And when they do encounter these conditions, they NEVER want to return to their weed-infested environment ever again.

As you consider this process, how much are you willing to invest? How committed are you to following through?

When we facilitate groups, we start with everyone in the room, and then we dismiss the executives so that we can have an authentically real conversation with front line staff. Sometimes we get initial negative feedback about leadership and resistance to collaborating, but I can't think of a time when we didn't eventually break through. It takes a willingness to suspend investment in your own ego and consider the other person's perspective, even when it may feel like the very last thing you feel like doing in that moment.

We aren't looking for leadership to dictate the agenda, because they tend to have a ten-thousand-foot view that doesn't necessarily capture the day-to-day reality. Starting with the line staff and then taking their observations back to leadership can be extremely challenging for executives to hear, but so necessary for their ability to shift from macro to micro levels of empathy and support.

UNITY in Action: StrongSpring Unpacks

An organization like StrongSpring could stay forever mediocre, have a less-than-average company, and never really encounter conflict. However, that lack of excelling and fulfilling potential creates its own inner conflict, doesn't it? If you're reading this book, I assume you want more.

That desire to raise yourself, your team, and your organization leads to an interesting problem: To improve, you need to put yourself out there. You need to risk some conflict, even though I'm teaching you to resolve it. So let me be clear... *some* conflict is necessary and, yes, should even be welcomed as a tool for sharpening and honing personal and cultural development. Within healthy guardrails and parameters, sometimes you need to tackle issues head on.

Recall the primary challenge Marley, the owner of StrongSpring, is facing—the conflict between employees and mid-level managers in the field and the home office. She understands this reality and decides not to overreact, although she is tempted to call all of the field ops' managers in and give them a piece of her mind. Instead, to *unpack*, Marley decides that rather than blaming her team in the field, she is going to look inward and consider her part in creating this contentious business climate.

Marley sits down at her desk for about thirty minutes and lists ten biases that she brings to the table in this volatile situation. She does so by writing each of these down on the left margin on a legal pad. At first, she finds herself getting upset because as she looks inward for her part in this chaos, she feels a natural tendency to blame others and a desire to scream from the rooftops, "Don't these people know what I've sacrificed to build this business?!" But she powers through, listing ten biases that helped lead to this scenario, one by one.

1   She believes she hired extremely competent people to run her field ops.
2   She believes she compensates them well.
3   She believes she has a reasonable expectation that well-paid competent employees can fix their own issues.
4   She believes that the explosion in early growth meant StrongSpring met the needs of customers.
5   She believes that internal company issues don't negatively impact external customers.

Marley continues with her last few biases until she comes up with a total of ten that she has written down meticulously on the left margin of her pad of paper.

After making the list, Marley sits back in her chair and studies it for a moment, feeling a host of emotions: thoughtful, angry, overwhelmed, frustrated. As she prepares to proceed to the next step in the UNITY path, she is also feeling something else that she hasn't in a long time about the conflict at hand.

A tiny bit hopeful.

Put It into Practice

After learning about the process of unpacking, revisit your two lists from earlier in this chapter. Can you go deeper? What (if anything) would you change now, and why?

What's Next?

The sacred work of UNITY is done by you, starting with the *unpacking* process and seeing yourself clearly. Once your journey of personal enlightenment begins, you will find yourself excited and enthusiastic in discovering where your once divergent paths will potentially meet. And when you do finally discern that ever-elusive mutuality, your relationship to that individual and to conflict management will never be the same again! You're not persuading anyone to perfectly agree with you, just finding common ground and a place where you can negotiate and compromise.

You might not be quite there yet, which is okay . . . and also a little bit by design. The next step, *navigate*, will move you closer toward your goal of deep personal connection and intentionality.

CHAPTER 4

STEP 2: Navigate

Growing up in Northern California, relatively close to the Sierra Nevada Mountain Range, we went skiing quite a bit as a family when I was young. On one of these outings when I was around ten or eleven, I had one of the scariest experiences of my life. Normally my dad would ski with us, but that morning, my older siblings and I ventured out while he stayed back at the lodge. My siblings wanted to ski down our "regular" hill, but I decided I wanted a bigger challenge and went off on my own. In retrospect, this was not only a really dumb idea, but I specifically remember my dad reminding us several times to stick together before heading out. So, instead of listening to his wise counsel, I proceeded to make another stupid decision: I ignored the Black Diamond signs (that represent dangerous and challenging terrain for advanced skiers only) and fueled myself on gusto and adrenaline. I was a good skier, but I wasn't Black Diamond good.

But that didn't stop me.

Hours after starting down the trail, I ended up way off the beaten path, lost and hurt. I was chest-deep in powder, the sun was setting, and I was crying, terrified and angry. I remember thinking I was going to die. Eventually, I was able to crawl my way (literally) to an area where another skier could faintly see me and hear my pleas for help.

Why was I so anxious to navigate my own path that I didn't listen to others? I thought. *Why didn't I listen to my dad, who told us to stick together?*

I'd ignored all the warning signs of trying to navigate alone, and I paid the price. I've kept that lesson with me all these years—which is why *navigate* means something a bit more communal as part of UNITY.

Taking Stock

In the *navigate* step, you are trying to understand what makes you and the other person different from a motivation and bias standpoint.

Here's what this looks like: In the *unpack* step, on the left side of the page, device, or whiteboard, you listed seven to ten of the biases and suppositions you bring to the feud you're currently working toward resolving by following each step of UNITY. You then did your best to list, on the right side, just across from your list, the seven to ten predispositions the other party maintains in this dispute.

In *navigate*, the goal is to go beyond the list and thoroughly define where each of your reasons comes from. What motivations and biases are underneath? In other words, what might each reason *mean*?

In the process, sometimes you realize that what bothers you about the other person's personality or approach doesn't actually stem from the current situation. It could be rooted in a lingering bias from a prior experience. By spelling everything out, the goal is to have a more academic, dispassionate, and objective viewpoint that gives you some perspective on what's happening, instead of getting swept up in the emotion.

Taking this unemotional inventory requires a great deal of work and intellectual honesty. In this step of navigating, you are still trying to get out of the one-sided emotional prism and objectively figure out your motivations and the other person's.

Put It into Practice

Revisit your lists from the unpack step.

Instead of listing reasons this time,

take an unemotional inventory of the biases

and motivations underneath those reasons.

For example, if a reason is,

"Nobody listens when I have good ideas,"

a bias underneath that may be,

"Every time I try to speak up, I'm not heard . . .

so what's the point?"

Complete this exercise for both your list

and their list.

Third-Party Input

A neutral confidant can be useful here. You want to choose someone who has nothing to do with the conflict. Try to find someone outside the organization who has no dog in the fight, so you know they aren't answering based on internal politics but rather giving their honest observations.

If you don't already have that kind of confidant, this is a wonderful opportunity to develop one and think about who could serve as a mentor in your life. Sometimes a spouse or partner can serve the purpose, but they generally have a bias toward your point of view and may not be able to point out your blind spots. For that reason, a third-party coach may be useful.

The best-case scenario is that the confidant will know both you and the other person in the conflict, without being beholden to internal politics or hierarchy. If you are struggling to find that person who is familiar with the situation and capable of rendering solid input and advice, I find that people in my orbit who are able to remain objective and levelheaded, no matter how dire or chaotic the situation, ALWAYS make superb thought-partners in situations just like this. When you spell out the situation to your confidant, do your best to capture both sides—the honest, unvarnished information you uncovered through *unpacking*. Doing so requires you to have a level of trust in the person you're telling so that you feel comfortable laying out the facts without feeling defensive or trying to vilify the other party. Why? Because without laying out the facts, you won't be able to *identify commonalities* in the next step.

Before you talk to a confidant, try to maximize your clarity about what you think the situation is. Get as far as you can on your own before opening yourself to outside opinions. That way, they can challenge you and ask you probing questions that move your understanding forward.

> ## *Put It into Practice*
>
> *Explain the situation to a trusted confidant, and show them both of your sets of lists. As a thought expansion exercise, ask them if there's anything you might be missing—and try your best to be fully open to hearing the answer.*

Building Empathy

Through the UNITY process, and particularly during the *navigate* step, we humanize the person who previously seemed like an opponent. The details of the differences matter less than the recognition that there will always be disparate ways of seeing things. Discrepancies don't need to trigger a sense of threat or emotional overload. From a place of curiosity and shared interest, we can mutually start to migrate to the middle, no matter what the issues are. It's about emotional positioning to ensure that you're seeing things the way that they truly are instead of the way your biases argue they should be. That's a place of clarity and possibility, not of competition. When you seek to understand, that's where it begins to become apparent that conflict is really 95 percent driven by emotion and issues themselves only account for the remaining 5 percent,

Think about that: Most conflict isn't about the actual positions themselves, just all the emotion we bring to them. When we invest in trying to understand another person's point of view, then by the time we go to *identify commonalities*, we've demonstrated that we're willing to do the work to get on the same page. Laying the foundation through these first two UNITY steps builds trust and shows consideration through your words, but especially and most importantly, your actions.

It's also important to acknowledge that at this point, even when thinking about the other person's point of view, we're still reflecting internally and making our best guess. We aren't cornering the other party and asking them what their motivations are.

As you've probably gathered by now, this work requires using and strengthening our empathetic side. Even if you can't fully flesh out the other person's motivations in the way *they* would describe them, at least by the time you're ready to speak to them, you've done the work of trying to take their point of view. That's a skill that increases with practice. The more you build that muscle and make it an intrinsic part of your life, the less arduous it feels to *unpack* and *navigate* the next time.

How to Understand Others' Positions That Might Differ from Your Own

Let's say you've *unpacked* and can see the value in this next step of *navigating*. However, maybe you're not sure how to start or what your own blind spots might be regarding your biases or others' perspectives. If you don't feel naturally inclined to gravitate toward other sentiments embedded in those with whom you're in active conflict, how can you prime that pump? Let's consider some steps that can be taken.

If you're feeling stuck when trying to think of the other person's point of view, I encourage you to reach out to others who may have valuable insights because that information may be helpful to take the next step. We've already covered the value of asking a trusted confidant what they think the other party's position might be if you aren't sure yourself. Another option is to list three to five people you know and would feel comfortable talking to who have successfully overcome conflict, have lived to tell about it, and have been a vessel to educate others about what they learned as a result of their collaborative success. From that list, start with the person you trust most, and set up a call to pick their brain about their approach. What has worked for them, and what would they recommend against? How did they find common ground in situations that initially seemed very polarized? See what inspiration you can take from their experience to apply to your own.

You can also read other books on this topic. I recommend *How to Have Impossible Conversations* by Peter Boghossian and James Lindsay, *Thinking Fast and Slow* by Daniel Kahneman, and *Empathy: Why It Matters, and How to Get It* by Roman Krznaric. If fiction is more your style, try *A Thousand Splendid Suns* by Khaled Hosseini, *Small Great Things* by Jodi Picoult, and *The Hate U Give* by Angie Thomas.

Tapping into that web of knowledge is simply part of the recipe for success. Using those combination of methods, you will ultimately break through. Once the UNITY process becomes second nature, you won't need to read up or talk to confidants every single time. However, those resources and thought partners can be useful the first time or two, if you feel at a loss. As you practice, you will no longer feel stuck and will be able to see both others' biases and your own. Keep consulting trusted partners as long as you want if it's helpful to you, but feel confident that the process will gradually become efficient and intrinsic if you stick with it.

Common Pitfalls and Pushbacks When Navigating

You may feel reluctant to *navigate* because you don't know whether your conjecture about the other person are 100 percent correct. I get that! The truth is that almost inevitably they may not be. That's okay.

The point isn't to be perfect; it's to harness your empathy, broaden your perspective, and expand your thinking to prepare for finding common ground.

People often say, "This sounds great, but how do I know I'm on the right track?" That's valid. You may not have deep knowledge of the person you're in conflict with. Your trusted advisor may not either. Still, by taking the time to brainstorm, reflect, and get impartial advice, you're ensuring a better chance of connecting with that person than if you predictably dug in with your own position.

Careful, though! A common pitfall is talking to too many "trusted advisors." When you have an abundance of people involved and contributing opinions, it can, and most likely will, heighten the drama. Navigating conflict in an empathetic, solutions-oriented way does require some discretion. Strategically choose the people you talk to, rather than using a shotgun approach. There needs to be alignment and intention.

At the same time, you don't want to rely soley on logic to the point that you don't take a moment, become a bit contemplative, and thoughtfully consider the best path forward. This process is designed to get some distance from the emotion—in that way, it strives to be black and white. But there are also always shades of gray around people's opinions and the exact approach you could take. Remain open to considering multiple possibilities about what the other person is thinking. None of them may be exactly right, but at least you have a place to start, rather than going in blind and without any reflection.

People often get nervous during the second step because they have a sense that listing biases in writing might get them in trouble. It can feel like official documentation and part of their permanent record that might expose them to liability. Remember, this is just a personal exercise for you. You're not trying to disparage another person—just the opposite, in fact. You're endeavoring to understand them, while at the same time, taking a human-centric approach You aren't putting this list in a personnel file; it's something you keep for yourself to help organize and guide your thinking.

There's also a "leap of faith" element at play here. You're spending all this time working on something that likely won't be 100 percent accurate. How do you even begin to know whether this level of mental and emotional investment is actually worthwhile and may even pay dividends? The secret is that you don't have to be completely accurate and you may actually never know, in some cases, what the impact of this process was for you and the other party in conflict. The exercise itself opens you up and shifts the narrative into a much more altruistic and less emotionally charged state. Even if you don't perfectly capture their point of view, you are getting out of your own opinions and looking at the situation from the person with whom you're in conflict vantage points, which humanizes the other party and defuses much of the oppositional dynamic. That's why this step is so essential and cannot, and should not, be entered into lightly.

Put It into Practice

Think about your personal and professional network, and consider who among them has successfully overcome conflict. Choose someone you're close to and trust, and ask if you can pick their brain about what worked for them and what didn't. Whether you find actionable takeaways or not, odds are that you've gained perspective and likely deepened a connection.

UNITY in Action: StrongSpring Navigates

After unpacking, Marley is ready to *navigate*. Having completed her list of ten internal biases that she brought to the table, she begins to make a similar list of perspectives, on the right side of that same legal pad, of what she believes that the field operators bring to bear in this situation. These include the possibility that her team didn't receive requisite training and resources that the home office should've provided to ensure success.

If only they knew how difficult it was to grow this company, she thinks, highly frustrated. *There just simply isn't enough time to train and equip these field ops like they want.*

She quickly realizes that thought is not a productive one, so she continues making her list. Maybe those in the field feel that employees in the home office are cliquey. It's possible that when they come to the home office for any reason, they may see it as though they're made to feel "less than" and left out of important company business.

Marley continues with her list until she has ten biases on the right to match the same number on the left. Though she's still more than a little skeptical about this process, she is committed to working the UNITY steps in order because she knows she needs to try something new if she has any hope of receiving a different outcome. In the next step that follows, she will *identify commonalities*.

What's Next?

The core of this work is emotionally driven self-discovery paired with the outside advice and support of mentors and trusted advisors. Almost every time, you will learn that your established confidants, in turn, have their *own* as well. You may also get reinforcement about what *not* to do along the way, which is critically important as we're considering deeply held beliefs such as motivations and biases.

In the next step, *identify commonalities,* you'll learn to go a bit deeper—and likely discover that you have more in common with the person you're in conflict with than you think.

CHAPTER 5

STEP 3: Identify Commonalities

don't know about you, but I *love* the Christmas holiday.
I mean, I really love it—the decorations, the food, the music, the family time. And when it comes to Christmas, I go big.

But let me back up.

Back in 2009, I accepted a new role I'd been offered at a health-care facility.

When I started, the operation had an absolutely horrific reputation. It possessed terrible regulatory results and was losing money, hand over fist, month after month. The departments weren't getting along, turnover was high, and the owners kept hiring and firing administrators. When I got there, though, the property itself felt somehow a bit magical. The building sat on an amazing seven-and-a-half-acre piece of land. I felt intrigued and saw huge potential in something that most people had written off. I set about hiring other people who recognized that same potential.

Often, it's tempting to write off conflict as unsolvable, deciding two people or two departments can never get along because there's too much damage, too many inherent hurdles, or not enough common ground. That was certainly the leadership's existing attitude toward the operation when I stepped in.

However, I came in with a very different vision. I didn't have every detail pinned down, but I felt like the company was located in an absolutely gorgeous location, making it a majestic little diamond in the rough. I was the executive director in charge of all the operations there, and because we were losing our shirts financially, I shook the tree more than anyone had in a long time. I let some bad apples go. It had to happen; the building had 176 beds but was only operating at 60 percent capacity, and we were not bringing in enough revenue by a long shot. The previous owner had sold the facility to the company that hired me. To their credit, even though they didn't have endless resources, they told me to do whatever I needed to do to succeed. I brought in a superstar marketer/assistant administrator, Rodney Zwahlen, and things started to look up almost immediately!

Still, I knew that we needed something sustainable that would differentiate us from the rest of our competition in the community. My first thought? Christmas, of course! The holiday that makes me incredibly sappy and nostalgic seemed like the perfect way to separate ourselves not just slightly, but on a massive scale. When I pulled together a committee to plan and organize a Christmas event, the team initially thought I meant a simple Christmas party for the staff. They had no way of knowing that I wanted to not just think outside the box; I was going to shatter that box into a million pieces.

I began that first planning meeting with a series of questions: "What if over the course of four or five days, we brought thousands of people in the community onto our property? And what if during that time, we completely transformed our campus into a magical winter wonderland, the likes of which they've never experienced? And what if Santa Claus came parachuting out of a plane each night, bringing joy, laughter, and cheer to the grounds of this business that so many had left for dead? What if we built a sleigh that could play movies through a huge sound system? What if we had a magical, live manger scene in the barn that we've always thought was an eyesore?"

People thought I was out of my ever-loving mind, but I had a vision. I wanted every single employee to dress up like they lived in Victorian England and speak with a Cockney accent, conjuring the feel of Charles Dickens. We'd have Mrs. Claus reading stories to the children and a twenty-foot-tall rocking horse with a spotlight on it where kids could sit and get their pictures taken. There would be artificial snow blowing in every imaginable direction; something people never see in that part of California. The first year, we spent about $150,000 on all the sets, decorations, Christmas lights, costumes, horse-drawn carriage rides, fancy entrées and desserts, and the merriest Christmas props you've ever laid eyes on.

The new owners backed me, because they realized if we could create a magical annual Christmas event—and if we could do it right—it could completely turn public perception around. Employees asked me how much we'd charge, but I said we wouldn't charge people a dime. To do so, I felt, would somehow cheapen this once-in-a-lifetime experience for members of our community. We wanted to draw them to the campus with an opportunity to enter their own "magic kingdom" a couple of hundred miles north of the "other one."

The first year, we brought in about 8,500 people over the course of four nights. The next year brought in over 10,000. We held the event from 2010 through 2013. Each year, though, the celebration grew, both in numbers of people attending as well as regional notoriety. By year two, it had grown to become the *it* family Christmas event in the entire region!

Positive operational results soon followed. The event helped increase our overall occupancy from 60% to 90% over the next six months. Revenue grew by $800,000 during that time. We dramatically improved our recruitment of nurses and licensed therapists, saw an immediate spike in employee retention numbers, and realized a 14 percent increase in employee and resident satisfaction during our next survey. The greater healthcare community began to stand up and take notice. Almost immediately, acute care providers in the region requested to tour our facility. We were also invited to host several key health fairs typically hosted by traditional hospitals. These healthcare providers recognized that we were an oasis full of dedicated professionals capable of giving patients in need an exceptional experience.

All these benefits came about because we brought people to where we were, opening their eyes to previously unseen services. And, above all, allowing them to experience what can only be described as a little Christmas magic.

The experience taught me an important lesson: Look past everything in front of you that says something can't work or be successful. Hello, conflict resolution!

And what made it possible, besides my unreasonable obsession with all things Christmas-y? *Identifying commonalities*, which allowed me to think outside the box. Although due to the rigorous demands of our entire staff in preparation for this annual holiday event, I did receive pushback from employees at times along the way. But at the end of the day, we had a similar goal: to find a way to help the company thrive. For them (and me), that meant job security and a larger potential for positive impact in the community. Building from that commonality gave us a place to grow from where we could have wasted energy butting heads.

When humans come together as they *identify commonalities*, often a beautiful symmetry begins to reveal itself. It takes faith and vision, but often you'll see previously untapped potential that can translate to business outcomes, sure. But the real win? Those are in the human outcomes.

How to Identify Commonalities

Now that you've *unpacked* and *navigated*, you have a list with two columns. At this point, it's time to *identify commonalities*. The first two steps have their "aha" moments, but this one is where you really start to find connection and pull everything together.

The goal is to *identify commonalities* between you and the person with whom you're in conflict. You've started looking at the person through a new lens, and now it's time for the next step! Begin by thinking internally how you can start to work together. Armed with clarity on your dual biases, you can start assembling the puzzle.

There are three stages to *identifying commonalities*:

1   Process the similarities, put them on paper, prepare for the dialogue, and feel empowered.

2   Process the differences, write down how you feel about the differences, and seek to understand what those differences mean.

3   Prepare to take ownership by generating some conversation starters based on what you learned in the stages above.

These stages are empowering because by working through them and writing down your thoughts, you can develop a sense of connection to the other person and ideas for broaching the subject of your conflict.

First, find the clearly analogous biases between your list on the left and the list of the other person's biases on the right and draw direct lines in between these two columns. Then, it's time to identify the less obvious similarities in biases and to draw lines connecting those as well.

Yes, if you haven't realized it by now, this process is not focused on continuing to anchor positions into areas of opposition. A major facet of UNITY is to continuously strive to turn assumed differences into opportunities that bridge divides and cement fractures that were deepened by two parties who, in many cases, forgot what the origins of their conflict were in the first place. Once you are able to find yourself in this open and honest headspace, your ability to dig deeper and find profound connections to two seemingly divergent positions can begin to be fully realized. The heavy lift is figuring out just how those differences actually may be, in fact, very closely aligned with what you assumed were completely incongruous from one another all along. It is only through this discovery that we can ultimately arrive at a place where commonalities have no choice but to rise to the surface and manifest themselves in very obvious and profound ways.

Maybe you and your colleague are at odds because of an unflattering rumor about them. Maybe they don't seem friendly in the brief interactions you've had. You then become anchored in your position of distancing yourself from them and making a choice to not be there in their "inner circle," or maybe you choose to not allow them in yours.

But then, perhaps through a situation where you find yourselves tied directly together on a work, school, or association project, you suddenly discover this person to be the antithesis of absolutely everything you imagined them to be. They are intelligent, kind, empathic. And, as has been the case many times throughout my life, you may even find mutual professional or personal compatibility and begin a path of true friendship and camaraderie.

This example is exactly how I feel about how we often approach supposed "differences" embedded within conflicts. At first, we buy into the fallacy that based purely on the input of others, many of whom we may even trust, or by limited personal examination of this individual, we treat their position on a particular issue as "not at our level" and therefore investing time in working on solutions would not be a wise or prudent move on our part.

I also used this analogy as a way to show just how closely aligned the notion that we are capable of painting a person with an unflattering brush when it's simply their position we disagree with and not necessarily anything to do with their character, integrity, or abilities. It's subtle but left unchecked, we can unknowingly wreck any potential to resolve substantial conflicts simply because we find it impossible to not attach the issue to the person. On one hand, since it is the other party who is espousing these positions, it may seem impossible to compartmentalize them separately. However, as we work toward growing savvier in how we approach UNITY, we become much more astute at re-examining issues that are divergent from our own, while at the same time validating the person who brought them to the table as thoughtful and intentional in their own right. This is a core and fundamental result of implementing UNITY in a genuine and intentional way.

Identifying commonalities, often by reverse-engineering and beginning at the places where our differences lie, allows you to meet the other person where they are, which sets you up for the next step—when you actually reach out to the other person and make contact.

By the time you're ready to start the conversation, you have much more to go on than just a list of biases and motivations; you have an understanding of the places where you're aligned and how those places can help you bridge the divide.

Put It into Practice

Review both of your lists you created in unpack *and* navigate, *this time specifically with the goal of pairing together the aspects of the lists that reveal common ground. Where are you similar? Take ample time to process.*

Sometimes the biases and motivations that seemed to be in conflict are actually much more similar than you first thought.

Here, you are likely to start internalizing the fact that as humans, we often have more similarities than differences—and that analyzing problems through that lens can feel so much more grounded and productive.

Guiding Questions

The idea here isn't to force a square peg into a round hole, but I acknowledge that it can feel like that if you're not used to this process. To give you a head start, begin by asking yourself some key questions:

- How do I view this person's differences?
- How can I make it work within this scenario?
- What is my approach going to be with this individual in terms of giving them grace and also trying to find understanding?

- What are our similarities?
- How can those similarities help us work toward a solution?

When you're ready to talk to the other person in the next step, you'll have information to share regarding what you've learned about your similarities and how what you thought were major divides were actually discussion points that have the potential to bring you together.

The truth is that you undermine your ability to handle conflict in a healthy way every time you pursue questions like these:

- What's in it for me?
- How is this impacting me negatively?
- Why doesn't this person understand me?

Instead of asking the above questions, the antidote is to build your conflict resolution muscles through questions like these:

- How can I better understand this other person?
- How can I have more empathy?
- How will their winning or their success ultimately lead to my success as well?

These reframed questions don't deny your right to want to get something positive out of the process. I'm simply advocating for putting those considerations second, after you've fully laid the groundwork to connect. The truth is, when you pursue success for others, it always comes back to you in some way. It's not a zero-sum game where for one person to win, the other has to lose. Conflict resolution is win-win.

The more you strengthen your resolution muscle by figuring out ways to solve conflict from the other person's point of view, the more you can facilitate those win-wins. The answer isn't always obvious or immediate, but you can find it.

It's very empowering to say, "Your success is also my success." It shows an investment in the world around you, and people respond to that investment. The more you actively work for others' success, the greater the success that comes back to you. It's not just personally gratifying but also the right thing to do. In turn, a rising tide lifts all boats.

The Power of Writing It Down

In the *identifying commonalities* phase, there's a lot of processing and internal dialogue. Write down your thoughts in the form of small lists for each stage, with three to five bullet points per list. Identify similarities, differences, and ideas for conversation starters. You don't need to go on for pages and pages—or if you do, end by distilling it to those three to five items for each stage. Sticking to that system organizes your thinking and allows you to be clear when you have the conversation.

Writing down your thoughts rather than just idly musing about these steps is important because it offers some emotional distance. If you can remove the hard feelings around some of your differences, you're more likely to come up with new ways to consider and value your similarities. Writing down your reflections also provides a visual sense of accomplishment.

I developed this system as a visual person who gains satisfaction from working through to-do lists. You may have a slightly different style and approach, which is okay, as long as you reach the outcome of organizing your thinking around your similarities and differences in a way that prepares you to communicate.

The point isn't just to generate a bunch of random thoughts but to *do* something with them. There needs to be a balance between pondering your position and theirs. If you're struggling here, you're not alone. Depending on the situation and your comfort with the process, some steps in UNITY may be more or less gut-wrenching, but in the end, it helps to leverage what you learned from each step before building with the next one. Reaching that place of clarity reinforces a sense of accomplishment and ownership, which I've seen time and time again in working with our clients. UNITY started for me as a passion project, but it became a proven system.

Put It into Practice

Review both of your lists you created in unpack *and* navigate, *this time specifically with the goal of examining the aspects of the lists that don't seem to line up. Where are you different? Take ample time to process.*

Sometimes the biases and motivations that seemed to be in conflict are actually much more similar than you first thought. Or sometimes, they're not.

Here, you are likely to start internalizing the fact that two things can be true at once. Analyzing problems through that lens—ironically, much like doing so when searching for similarities—can feel so much more grounded and productive.

Common Ground

One of my clients who experienced a breakthrough did a review of past successes with a difficult person, reflecting on when they were most and least approachable. They remembered having attended a church event years earlier with their families and connecting over the fact that they both had kids who were struggling. That conversation created a point of meaningful connection, but my client had completely forgotten about it. After taking that very human moment into account, by the time they moved into the next step of UNITY, they'd cleared up the conflict in a single phone call. They realized they'd been holding the other person to a ridiculous standard that they couldn't meet themselves. By remembering the shared challenge with their kids, they reframed and decided being right in the conflict was not the most important thing to them. This is the kind of glue that holds organizations—and relationships—together in conflict.

Of course, you won't always have a longstanding relationship, but if you feel stuck regarding your commonalities, think back on everything you've experienced together. Were there any moments that bonded you or at least surprised you about them? What do you know about the person outside of this conflict?

Based on these reflections, you can come up with some possible conversational gambits:

- "Do you remember the time we [fill in the blank with shared experience that demonstrates a point of connection]?"
- "I think we're about 80 percent aligned, and I'd love to hear what you think about the differences that remain."
- "What would be your ideal outcome in this situation?"

Remember, in conflict, it's 5 percent the issue and 95 percent the emotions surrounding it.

Common Pitfalls and Pushbacks When Identifying

During this step, it's important to avoid complaints or insinuations about the positions that you don't agree with. You may be wondering, "How can I avoid the temptation of inserting my own thoughts into what the other person may be feeling in order to find common ground?" Empathy takes practice. I encourage you to go back to the previous step and refresh your memory of the other's biases, motivations, and potential point of view. Without editorializing or modifying where they seem to be coming from, brainstorm as many possibilities as you can think of regarding how their positions align with, resonate, or are similar to yours.

In applying this process, I periodically remind myself that there's no guarantee every item on the lists will align, but by genuinely investing the effort to find the alignment, I guarantee my view of the other person will be far more sympathetic. As a consequence, I expand the potential for resolution. If we dig in and stick with our patterns that haven't worked, we simply guarantee that we'll get the same result, or in some cases worse.

If you go through this step and decide you aren't actually committed to meeting in the middle, that's your prerogative, but know that doing the same things won't get you different results. If you're okay with your current outcomes, then I genuinely wish you well. But if you'd rather master the ability to truly put someone's success before your own, and in turn have them migrate toward wishing for your success, then this foundational shift is for you. When you stick with it, UNITY is gratifying and deeply impactful.

That means even though deep down you may want to rush through this step and stay surface level, take the time to work through it with patience. The more you commit to it without rushing, the more value it will yield. Before you move on to the next step of *taking ownership*, internalize what you've identified as deeply as possible. The point isn't to check a box and call the other person as quickly as you can—it's to clarify and change your way of thinking.

In fact, I advise sleeping on this step for at least twenty-four hours and even longer if necessary. Talk to your trusted confidant about it and see if they have any additional ideas or perspective to add. The system doesn't take years—it's efficient—but don't rush.

Once you've fully *identified commonalities*, it's time to make the call.

Put It into Practice

Prepare to take ownership *by generating some conversation starters based on your assessment of your similarities and differences. You don't want the upcoming conversation to feel rehearsed, rather your aim is to be thoughtful and prepared.*

UNITY in Action: StrongSpring Identifies

With her list complete of her own biases in the left margin and those of her field operations team on the right, Marley is ready to *identify commonalities*. She begins to examine each one of these biases critically, both in the left margin and right. She does so for a very specific reason: She is beginning to parcel out which of these biases are actually more similar than they are different.

For example, with her own personal bias of "resenting field ops staff because they don't fully understand the sacrifice that she has made to build this business," Marley suddenly realizes that in the right margin, she has listed one of the field ops' predispositions to be: "We don't often feel recognized and heard for the contributions we are making daily to ensure success."

Wait, Marley thinks, a little bit astonished. *We actually want the same thing—to be seen and heard as having a part in the overall success of the company.*

She draws a line directly between these two biases, connecting them as like-minded. She continues this exercise until six of the ten biases in both the left and right margins are connected because of their similarities.

We're struggling with so many of the same things, Marley thinks, a smile beginning to form on her face. *We want to be on the same track, but the trains are going in opposite directions. I need to be the one to get everyone on board and moving together if we're going to fix this once and for all.*

What's Next?

I know you picked up this book for a reason. You don't want to just win in conflict; you want to feel a true sense of purpose, meaning, and accomplishment. The way to get there is through mutual understanding and the extension of grace, which we can get to if we learn to *identify commonalities*.

Next, we'll explore how to *take ownership*—and why the ability to do that is so important. Not just to resolve conflict, but to grow and progress as people.

CHAPTER 6

STEP 4: Take Ownership

In the fall of 1998, I was nearly finished with my master in public administration (MPA) degree at California State University, Fresno. In lieu of writing a master's thesis, I elected to take five comprehensive examinations. This option was absolutely no joke—the material, at times, went back a couple of years, so a big part of my studying was also reviewing and relearning highly technical material. To receive my degree, I needed to pass all five exams on the first go-round—no exceptions, no excuses.

There was only one problem: At the time, my life situation wasn't exactly conducive to dropping everything and studying like a madman for these exams. I was incredibly busy with my demanding job in healthcare, and my wife and I had a toddler and a baby. If I didn't pass each of these exams, I would have to drag my degree out another semester or perhaps even be dropped from the program—something that would cost my family personally and financially.

For two weeks, I spent every waking hour of "free time" cramming, doing everything possible to prepare. Then, it was time: I had three days to complete five exams. On some questions, I felt a little lost. On a great majority, though, I felt grounded in what I knew, like all those hours of studying had paid off. Essentially, for those three days, I oscillated between feeling proud of all the effort, time, and energy I'd put forth on one end of the spectrum to a feeling of hopelessness and dread on the other.

The professors graded each test by hand because many of the responses were essay questions and well, let's face it . . . it was 1998 and "snail mail" in higher education was still very much a thing. I became obsessed with checking my mailbox, waiting for those results to come. And they did, within about a month—well, four out of five of them did, anyway.

Pass, pass, pass, pass.

Only one to go. Day in and day out, I'd go to the mailbox hoping for the results of that fifth and final comprehensive exam, the one in Dr. Cha's class. As weeks dragged on, I was starting to get worried not only that I'd probably failed but also that if I didn't get the results soon, I was going to have to stay (and pay) to continue the program for another semester—the last thing my wife or I wanted, or could afford, at the time!

Finally, I couldn't wait any longer. I called the professor, Dr. Marn Cha.

"Yes, I would love to talk to you about your exam," Dr. Cha said. "Come to my office."

Come to your office? I thought. *I'm done for.*

When the day arrived, I wasn't sure what to expect or why an in-person meeting was necessary. But after a bit of small talk, Dr. Cha got to the point.

"Brandon, what you put together was really good," Dr. Cha said. "I would have passed anyone else with this, but I know that you can do better. I would like you to write me a ten-page essay going further into the concepts on the exam, due in two weeks."

What the heck? I thought. *This isn't fair. I checked all the boxes. This program needs to be done so I can move on with my life.*

"Thank you for explaining, Dr. Cha," I said. "But I don't understand. You just told me you would pass other people. Are we creating two different standards here?"

"My job is to look at what people are individually capable of," he said. "But this is not your best effort, so I cannot give you a passing grade."

I left that office more annoyed and angrier than I'd been in a long time, but I wrote the paper. It was a team effort; Kathryn proofread it for me and over a quarter of a century later, I still remember her telling me, "Honey, this is REALLY good!" A few days after I submitted it, Dr. Cha called me into his office again. He would not tell me the results on the phone, a bit of déjà vu.

"This is outstanding work," he said. "But you have more in you. I want you to try again, this time a twenty-page paper."

I was livid, knowing this would mean I would have to stay another semester. I even became a little obstinate in his office, although I was at least smart enough to know not to say anything that would get me booted from the program, right then and there in my professor's office.

As I poured myself into yet another paper, I called friends and colleagues, complaining about Dr. Cha. I was, for lack of a better word, pissed. My wife and I had very little money at the time. I was just starting my career. I was missing time with my young family—time I desperately wanted. For what? Because *this guy* kept stringing me along.

After grinding the paper out, I turned it in triumphantly. Dr. Cha called me a couple of days later, asking me—you guessed it—to come into his office.

"Brandon, this will be the last time," he said. "I'm not even going to give you a page count or put you in any sort of box. I want you to come back in two weeks with a paper that tells the story of what you learned from this course. And I want you to defend it orally."

I do not have words to describe my level of disappointment and anger in that moment, which must have shown on my face. It felt like I was now doing a hybrid of exams AND a thesis. *Why?* I thought. *How is any of this fair?*

"Brandon, let me be very clear… it's pass or fail this time around, and this will be your last attempt."

There was almost an empathy in his voice then, a lot of emotion. He surely knew the suffering he was causing me, yet he was standing firm.

"What you've produced is some of the best work I've seen," he said. "I can see all these progressing versions of you in this work. Now, I need your very best version!"

Two more weeks. One more paper. A lot more calls to friends and anyone who would listen about how unfair the situation truly was— and how the awful Dr. Cha was the director of the whole debacle. At one point, I even considered going to the dean to complain.

When the time finally arrived and as I began my oral arguments defending my paper, I clearly had an edge to me because of what I had been put through over the course of many months. All the pent-up feelings that I'd bottled inside of rage, resentment, and disdain for Dr. Cha spilled out, but not directly. I was able to channel the fire and passion, funneling it directly into the course material and content in a most vigorous and forceful way.

When I finally concluded, and the smoke ultimately cleared (I firmly believe there was actual smoke that I emitted that day), something extraordinary happened: Dr. Cha leaned back in his chair, folded his arms, looked straight up to the ceiling for what seemed like a minute and a half, and then finally shot a gaze directly at me. I've never felt such tension in my life. It truly was an astonishing moment in which the stakes could not have been any greater. I was either being awarded my graduate degree right then and there or walking out of his office a fractured and broken man.

"Congratulations, Brandon," he said. "This is absolutely the best version of you. The reason I put you through this is because I knew that in the confines of this material, you had the potential to do some of the best work I've ever seen. And I was getting great work, but it wasn't the best work I've ever seen. *This* is. You've passed."

He began to get a little emotional, and I followed suit. In the moment, I had to *take ownership* internally. Dr. Cha had stated a principle that is eternal, one I believe in wholeheartedly: that we should give the best of ourselves, absolutely our best effort . . . *especially* in adversity. There are no shortcuts or easy roads to achieve the success we desire. *We* have to reach out and take advantage of the opportunities in life that are presented to us. We also have to extend our best efforts to meet those rare moments of fortuity and never had that lesson been more profoundly hammered into me, than it was that winter night by Professor Marn Cha. And then, as if the universe couldn't teach me any more life lessons, it suddenly washed over me, and I realized in an instant that when I complained to all who would listen about how unfair my experience was in finishing my master's program, it was actually *ME* who was the problem. Dr. Cha could not have been more spot on . . . I was so busy feeling sorry for myself that I neglected to recognize that only when I dug deeper than I ever had to locate what I didn't know existed, that I actually stumbled upon one of the greatest lessons that I may ever encounter; when we give maximum effort in search of something not yet known, we will find treasures previously undiscovered.

In a matter of minutes, I'd gone from hating Dr. Cha to respecting him more than just about anyone I've ever known. In fact, we've stayed in touch, and he is my close friend and mentor to this day. He taught me that we can be angry and in conflict for 99 percent of the race, but that last one percent—the final few yards—is where the magic can happen if we have paid the price to put ourselves in the best possible position to receive it. This realization impacted me profoundly then, and it has transformed me every day since in some way, informing my work, my relationships, and just about every other facet of my life.

If that's not the very definition of *taking ownership*, then I would be hard pressed to come up with anything in the same stratosphere even remotely close. I've seen its power over and over again in my life. In my experience, the *take ownership* step is the one when the manna from heaven rains down, and suddenly all the pieces come together in an unforeseen epiphany. There's a sense of figuring things out that you couldn't access before.

Ready? Let's go.

Reaching Out with Openness, not Manipulation

Taking ownership is as important a step as there is within UNITY as it ushers in the moment where, after engaging in so much of the innate self-discoveries, where you finally establish contact with the other party. You're not manipulating anyone, tricking them into agreeing with you, or projecting onto the other person. The goal of this step is centered in altruistic motives and if it begins to feel less unselfish, it's worth a lookback into the *identify commonalities* phase to ensure that you internalized those common denominators you both share. Reflecting back on the issues that unite and letting go of those that divide is the only way forward.

The true objective in resolving conflict is not to reach perfect agreement on one-hundred percent of issues; rather, it's to find symmetry, unified purpose, and understanding that were not previously there. When people are aligned, that's a conversation, not a conflict. And that's what we're going for.

Connection and transformation are much more likely when you have meaning and purpose. The step of *taking ownership* is when you figure out your "why." The process starts with the "what"—resolving differences—but then you need to know *why* you're making the effort. *Why* do you need to come together? As UNITY becomes second nature, you and the other person will likely start learning things about each other that you hadn't known previously, and you'll begin to put to bed notions that you'd long held onto about this person, but are just now discovering to be patently untrue and inaccurate.

Sounds wonderful, right? It is—but it takes a whole lot of work, a focused level of reflection, and an abundance of good old-fashioned patience. The patience piece is especially important because when you're facing an uncomfortable dispute with a coworker, sibling, or a friend, it can be tempting to jump straight to the conversation. But the groundwork is what makes the difference. *Taking ownership* is not forced or coerced, even though one person is generally spearheading the interaction, and it's rare to reach "enlightenment" at the exact same time.

In my experience, once people figure out their "why" and tap into their greater purpose, they feel excited to embrace the way forward. They have a new set of lenses, and suddenly the "what"—the details of the disagreement—doesn't matter in the same way.

When people are open to the process, it works. Sometimes clients come to our coaching sessions biased against the possibility of UNITY working, which, ironically, can become a self-fulfilling prophecy. But when you engage in an honest, open way, it's possible to move beyond entrenchment and deep-seated resentment. To *take ownership*, you need to at least compartmentalize, if not fully let go of the feelings of resentment.

When you do, you'll be willing to reach out and connect with the other person. *Taking ownership* doesn't mean labeling yourself wrong and terrible or taking all the blame. Doing so would only open you up to getting stepped on or exploited. The person you're reaching out to doesn't always start from a place of intellectual or emotional honesty with themselves, either. If you prostrate yourself, it can simply validate their biases and self-righteousness rather than inspiring analysis.

Now, you can't force that person to have a nirvana moment and recognize your commonalities. However, *taking ownership* in a balanced way and initiating contact opens up that possibility—which is what this entire process is built upon.

Handling the Logistics

Since you're initiating the conversation, play to your strengths. Approaching the dialogue in an inauthentic or unprepared way can crater the entire process. Even if you have a misstep, there's still value in trying, but I encourage you to proceed as thoughtfully as possible. Here are a few logistical considerations to keep in mind.

Meet in Person

In-person contact isn't always realistic, but it is ALWAYS the best. Even if you have to drive an hour or two or make other arrangements to be in front of this person, it is invariably the most effective choice. Looking directly into someone's eyes gives you a window into their soul and their sincerity.

If you want proof, look no further than COVID. The pandemic showed many of us that we took in-person interactions for granted, including their relationship to defusing conflict. There's a power to being in the same room with someone that goes beyond intellectual understanding. Even if you say the exact same words, the effect is different over a video call, on the phone, or in an email. Being face-to-face heightens your ability to resolve issues.

Let me tell you a little story about why this principle is so powerful to me. My daughter, Natalie, recently got married. She's almost six feet tall, and her husband, Luke, is six-foot-seven, so we expect their kids to be future NBA and WNBA players (one can dare to dream). She was always an excellent volleyball player and swimmer. The response to COVID in schools in California was particularly aggressive. Kids in all grades were not allowed to attend classes in-person, and sports and practices were strictly forbidden. You already know I spent a substantial amount of time in my career in the field of healthcare. I saw a fair amount of deaths related to COVID, so I took it seriously. At the same time, I saw so many negative consequences for my daughter in not being allowed to continue with school, see friends, and play sports during lockdown.

As she continued to be deprived of in-person connection due to the circumstances of the pandemic, it drove Natalie into a highly unstable place. She developed a severe eating disorder that sent her to the hospital and almost killed her. We stayed by her side throughout her time at University of California, San Francisco (UCSF) Benioff Children's Hospital. When she was finally discharged, Natalie's only option was Telehealth, virtual FaceTime therapy sessions, which were not nearly as effective as in-person treatment. The isolation and shutdown of activities in her life exposed anxiety which took a path of restricting food to solve her mental anguish.

Fortunately for us, there was a happy ending. Natalie is our warrior girl, and today, she's become an advocate who shares her experience with anorexia to help others. I'm endlessly proud of her! It also turned my wife, Kathryn, into a fearless protector for those who struggle with eating disorders as well as both of us into ardent critics of the seemingly eternal trend to continuously push diet culture and illogical expectations of body types. The entire experience was horrific, but we were unified in rallying around our daughter and experienced firsthand what can happen when people come together in the face of adversity.

I share that story to celebrate Natalie, certainly. But it also illustrates that in general, COVID showed many of us that we couldn't possibly comprehend how much we needed each other in ways large and small. If you truly can't *take ownership* in person, then it won't tank the whole process, but you'll give yourself a greater likelihood of success if you can meet face to face.

Be Organic and Authentic

This conversation should be authentic, which means it can't feel rehearsed. Counterintuitively, it *does* take intention to prepare. Practice, but don't allow it to become so robotic. Give the interaction plenty of thought in advance, but ultimately come to the exchange ready to have an open, responsive, reciprocal, and improvisational conversation.

To get into the right head space, consider asking a trusted ally, like a family member or longtime friend, to help you understand when you were most organic in your true self and how you showed up. This likely isn't the same person you'll consult about your blind spots in the conflict. It may seem like hard work to consult others in preparation for your conversation, but stubborn disputes that could negatively impact your career or family over the long term deserve the effort. UNITY is not about quick fixes. Sometimes disagreements do resolve quickly, but we need to be willing to put in the time required.

There's a side benefit to consulting someone about when you've been most grounded in your authentic self: Generally speaking, the narratives you hear back will build your confidence with reminders of your best attributes and abilities. Because the feedback is based in concrete instances they've observed, you can trust the message and let it sink in. It's also affirming and helps you feel equipped to embark on a challenging conversation.

Getting that outside perspective is valuable because accurate self-assessment can be challenging to say the least. We can be our own worst critics, particularly if we're feeling nervous or vulnerable about a conflict. This part of the process isn't about rehearsing; it's about preparing, which is an important distinction.

Sometimes, you'll have funny conversations with your trusted advisors too. One client told me he's always admired his dad and reached out to him for perspective. His dad turned out to be grateful and proud he was calling for a meaningful purpose, rather than to borrow money! The participant described the conversation with his dad as life-changing. There are mutual benefits to seeking someone out as a mentor, and it has a tendency to deepen the relationship in beautiful and unexpected ways.

As the meeting approaches, prepare, but don't get so wrapped up in practicing all the details that you stop being present and genuine. As you talk to people you trust who know you well, focus not on the perfect thing to say but rather on what opens you up to empathy.

Be Present

As you approach the conversation, come in with the frame of mind that you'll stay in the moment and not project your prior experiences on the person you're in conflict with. You're trying to have a clean slate. In that moment, nothing else matters beyond seeking understanding with the person directly in front of you.

Listen for similarities between what you unpacked regarding biases, commonalities, and discoveries and what they're conveying to you. They might agree with or amend what you thought, both of which are okay. Not just in theory, but in principle, doing so sets the stage for an open and honest conversation in which you are committed to listening intently, not interrupting, and using body language that signals your interest and openness.

Your job is to communicate in every way possible that what they say matters. Simply signaling that investment often breaks down walls that have been in place for weeks, months, or years. Again, it's not manipulation; it's genuine investment in transformation and resolution, which naturally happens when you connect in a new way. The old barriers start to melt.

Focus on "We"

As an opener, avoid "I believe," "I feel," or "I want you to know." Studies indicate that those phrases put people off and don't lead to conflict resolution, in part because excessive "I" statements can signal a lack of empathy. That might seem counterintuitive, since there are strands of psychology that emphasize always saying "I" rather than "you," though that is more in relation to accepting personal responsibility rather than initiating collaboration.

The issue is if you're already at odds, "I" can sound accusatory. It's not that you have to avoid ever saying "I" through the whole conversation; for instance, you might say, "I understand what you're saying" or "I had a wonderful thought about you." Overall, though, UNITY emphasizes using "we" to avoid signaling separation or discord between two parties. In general, I think about saying "we," "our," or "us" four to five times for every one instance of "I."

Be Patient

Patience, as they say, is a virtue . . . and it definitely holds true at this stage. Remember, you're going into this conversation having thoughtfully prepared, whereas the other person is going in cold. They need time to understand and get on board if they're willing. They won't always warmly receive the invitation.

When you make the overture to find common ground, expect to receive a range of responses. One end of the spectrum is, "Hey, this is great. I'm willing to try." The other end is, "I don't agree with what you're saying, and I don't actually understand how you think we are on common ground."

If you receive the latter response, try to tap into understanding. You can state that you initially didn't see any common ground either, and your realizations didn't happen overnight. You spent some time reflecting on how they were feeling and how that informed the differences between you, and you empathize with their position.

Remember, the "what" matters much less than the "why." For instance, to bridge differences, you might need to acknowledge that their department's focus is money, while yours is customer service. You can then bridge that *what* to a *why*—you both want the company to succeed, and great customer service also drives revenue. The two interests don't have to be in competition. They can have different metrics but share a common goal.

Don't Make Assumptions or Prescriptions

You don't get to prescribe the resolution. You can *take ownership*, but you can't dictate the place the two of you end up. Trying to do so makes assumptions without shared evidence. You've done the work of unpacking yourself, but you can't presume to know exactly what's going on for the other person.

They also need time to process. Unilaterally skipping ahead to the end point ignores their agency and can come across as insulting, which only escalates the conflict.

Put It into Practice

As you prepare for the conversation, consider reaching out to a trusted friend or colleague and ask them to help you understand when you were the most organic in your true self. Ask them how you showed up in that moment— what worked, and what didn't? Use that feedback with intention as you prepare for your conflict-addressing conversation.

Elements of Success and Examples

I know you're wondering, *What do I say first? What is the script?* Hopefully by now, this far into the book, you realize that THERE IS NO SCRIPT. Open the conversation by focusing on your discoveries, enthusiasm, and commitment, not the substance of the conflict. Every conversation starts differently, and your approach needs to be organic to your specific situation.

To give you a sense of how such an exchange might start, here are some examples of what someone in your position might say to the person you are at odds with:

- "How great is it that we're here together today."
- "Thank you for taking the time and allowing us to share together."
- "We've had some challenges, our share of disagreements, and it's really caused me to act in a way that's not naturally who I want to be."
- "This is not who I am with other people, and it's certainly not who I want to be in our relationship."
- "I've realized lately that I was so entrenched in viewing something in a way totally opposed to how you were viewing it. As I organized my thoughts, I actually went as far as making a map of where our similarities were and where our differences still remained. We're not 100 percent aligned on everything, but I realized more unites us than divides us. Can I share what I found with you, not in any way for you to exactly agree with my viewpoint, but to see if any of my discoveries may be a surprise to you?"
- "Hey, I know I'm hitting you with a lot. I'm super excited about this, and forgive me for being overly enthusiastic, but I learned something that I never realized before. It was 100 percent about

myself and how I was approaching things. The reason I'm even reaching out to you is I previously viewed your approaches as an impediment to my success. Now I've realized not only is that not true, but your success will ultimately lead to mine. Here's why. I know this is a lot for you to digest, which is totally understandable. And I want you to have a chance to really think about this instead of feeling compelled to respond to my question right now."

As far as the dialogue, I recommend three things:

- **Reach out enthusiastically.** For example: "Hey, Bob, I made this discovery while thinking about our differences on this issue that I'm really excited about, and I wanted to share it with you."
- **Share the reason.** For example: "I immediately thought of you in this scenario because of how different our viewpoints have been and because I realized how closely aligned we could become."
- **Don't assume they'll be enthusiastic right away; ask for feedback.** For example: "I would love to know how far off my impression is compared to yours and what your thoughts are."

Whatever you say, focus on the discoveries you've made and the goal they're leading you toward. The idea is to communicate that you've had some self-reflection and want to conduct yourself in a different, more enlightened way than ever before.

Overall, when individuals approach this process with openness, collaboration, and "we"-oriented language, highly positive feedback is generally received regarding the process from the other party who was invited to be a part of a new way forward with UNITY. Of course it doesn't always hit the mark, but generally when we analyze why, we see a breakdown somewhere in fully implementing the steps.

Essentially, you're taking responsibility for the discoveries you're sharing while leaving room for the possibility that you may have made incorrect assumptions about the other party. What you've uncovered provides a launch point, not a final verdict. Approaching the conversation with absolute certainty will turn people off. Instead, you're sharing a hypothesis and inviting them to collaborate.

Some participants have suggested that asking for feedback might just open the door for the other person to tell you you're wrong. Well, maybe you are. The point isn't to win and be right; it's to share your interpretation as a means of connecting. The goal is to create a respectful, open environment that organically allows for *"light bulb moments."* You initiate the process and ask questions, and they engage in response. It's not about conceding anything but rather taking steps forward toward resolution if possible. What you've uncovered provides a launch point, not a landing zone.

Put It into Practice

Reach out to the person or team you've been in conflict with and ask to have a conversation. Schedule it carefully, giving yourself enough time to thoughtfully structure the logistics and prepare.

It's Not Worth Being a Jerk

I once read an article that completely flipped my way of thinking about why we do things in life or in business. It gave the example of needing to fire an employee. You have a choice in that moment. You could be kind, thanking them for their time and apologizing that it didn't work out. Or, you could be vindictive, saying something like, "You've been terrible for this organization. You've been late. You didn't treat people right. You didn't do your job well. Here's your check. Get out of here."

The article shared that most people don't learn to be kind in moments of terminating someone's employment, or if they hear that they should, they don't think about *why*. The truth is, there's a business case for kindness. If that person files a complaint for wrongful termination, you've muddied your case and made your position more difficult. Another cost of being a jerk is creating enemies. You might get a short-lived high from speaking your mind and telling someone off because it makes you feel strong or powerful. However, that person is now more likely to retaliate, amplifying your problems.

Deeper than that, though, ethics is about acting in a certain way simply because it's the right thing to do.

How you treat people in life determines your opportunity to have productive conversations in the future. When you go your separate ways, you don't have to be lasting enemies. In some cases, now is simply not the right time to work together, but later might be. Being able to separate current fit from future potential is an underrated skill.

I used to follow the opposite playbook, based on what I'd learned from my first professional mentor, Dick. I'd sometimes give people a piece of my mind on their way out the door. Today, though, even if I see someone as deserving to be fired, I try my very hardest to be kind and empathic. I don't give them a laundry list of critiques. Instead, I say, "I'm so sorry it didn't work out. I absolutely wish you the best, and if there's anything I can do to help you in your future employment, I'm here for you." That offer stands no matter who the person is.

People have actually started crying in relief in those moments, telling me when I hand them their final check that they were expecting me to yell at them. Some have given me a hug on the way out the door, just because I treated them with basic humanity and respect. I'm not a saint for meeting that baseline; it's a sign that those qualities are unfortunately too rare in business today.

You never know the true cost of being a jerk. Your behavior could follow you for years to come. A person you mistreat could tell ten of their friends never to patronize your company, and the negative reputation ripples outward.

What does this have to do with UNITY? By the time you *take ownership*, it needs to be about opening space and then turning over the conversation, not dominating the other person, forcing them to respond in a certain way, or making a dramatic statement. Your humility increases the chance that they will share your interest in reaching understanding because they'll see you as a human being with a different perspective rather than one who can't be trusted.

When you devote full sincere attention to each of the steps, you maximize the chances that the other person *will* meet you somewhere in the middle. They'll likely have an interest in understanding where you're coming from, even if they don't agree. And while that's true, I encourage you to go into the conversation being okay with the possibility of not getting your way. You're going to share what you will and in turn listen to what they choose to reveal. The value of the process cannot be contingent on achieving a particular outcome. Stay open to being surprised . . . because you just might be.

Put It into Practice

As you start the conversation, remember that the other person doesn't have the same understanding of why you're both there. That means after you start, your biggest job is to stay present and actively listen. Do not interrupt, and do not give in to the temptation to say, "Yes, but . . ."

And above all, remember that the value of the UNITY process is not contingent on any particular outcome.

Common Pitfalls and Pushbacks When Taking Ownership

Now, it's true that in certain circumstances, a person who is approached for reconciliation by a party who is putting into practice the steps of UNITY may not do so willingly. They may also possess motives that are not pure and in rare cases, may even try to take advantage of your kindness and desire to come together. Sometimes, clients will say something like this: "I approached them in what I thought was a gracious manner. I went through the steps in very intentional ways, and yet the other person took advantage of my generosity and willingness to come together. They took it as an opportunity to walk all over me." In the vast majority of cases when people have come to me with these unfortunate accounts, I've found that they, in general, treated UNITY in an "à la carte" fashion: picking and choosing which steps they preferred and completely omitting some other points altogether.

Not everyone will be in the right headspace to respond to your invitation to participate in UNITY, even if your efforts in reaching out are genuine and with good intent. However, in my experience, it is far more likely that poor outcomes when initiating UNITY occur as a result from a misunderstanding of the steps within the framework. Sadly, in many of these cases that I've examined, there was incredible potential to have productive conversations that could've led to a full reconciliation. And even if you did find that the other person ultimately wasn't responsive, that wouldn't negate the value of doing the work to understand them and be more empathic to their particular circumstance.

I'm giving you permission to be ok if the UNITY framework doesn't work as you had hoped it would for the following reason: You've gained a much broader and deeper perspective of how your interests align and intersect with each other. Those realizations can continue to inform your conduct, no matter what other people decide to do. Yes, you'd love for them to meet somewhere in the middle, but this process isn't about leading people by the nose or making them do what you think is the right thing. It's about growing through shared humanity. No matter what happens, if you commit and follow through, I promise you one thing: you will assuredly reap many rewards!

UNITY in Action: StrongSpring Takes Ownership

After *identifying commonalities*, Marley knows that she finally needs to do something about this perilous situation. Left unchecked, it could easily torpedo all that she and her team have built.

To *take ownership*, Marley writes down on her legal pad the key people that she needs to reach out to in order to gain perspective:

- Jane, VP of Field Ops, because of her extensive oversight and influence in the field.
- Norah, Chief Operating Officer, because she needs to be part of the solutions that bridge home office to field operations.
- Charlie, Chief People Officer, because if this change is going to be sustainable and effectively communicated throughout the organization, he will play a key role in making this happen.
- Autumn, who oversees logistics as Director of Supply Chain. Marley knows just how intertwined Autumn's efforts are within the fabric of the organization. Without her buy-in, there will be zero chance for success.
- Chloe, Executive Coordinator and truly Marley's Chief of Staff in every possible way. Not a thing happens in the company without Chloe knowing about it, and Marley owes a massive amount of StrongSpring's success to Chloe for managing countless moving parts simultaneously, while somehow not losing her mind in the process.

List complete, Marley calls each one to invite them to an in-person meeting she is planning the coming week, following up with a calendar invitation and a note thanking them for taking the time for this important event.

Before the appointed day and time arrives, Marley seeks to deepen her level of knowledge about these key members of her team, especially a couple of them whom she doesn't know quite as well as the others.

Who knows all of these people the best? Marley wonders. Almost as soon as she asks herself the question, she knows the answer: *Chloe. She really makes it her business to get to know each and every employee of the company on a granular level. I need to meet with her ASAP.* Chloe is more than an employee to Marley. She is a true confidant and a friend. As part of her preparation for the executive-team meeting, Marley does a deep dive with Chloe to ensure that they're both in complete and total lockstep with the individual concerns and challenges that these key employees are experiencing.

In that in-person two-hour meeting with Chloe, Marley shares her desire to *take ownership* of her part of these challenges which have loomed large within StrongSpring and seeks perspective from Chloe. In this meeting, Marley gains not just an increased understanding of how valuable these team members are to the company but also a critical appreciation for who they are as people, separate from just their roles as employees.

Though she has not yet spoken to a single one of the other team members about what weighs heavy on her mind and heart, Marley feels more connected to them than ever. With all of this groundwork laid, she feels vastly more prepared for the in-person meeting with the rest of those on her list.

A few days later, Marley greets Jane, Norah, Charlie, Autumn, and Chloe as they walk into the conference room for the meeting, deeply appreciative for their willingness to adjust their schedules to take part in what she believes will be a momentous shift in the direction of StrongSpring.

Marley begins the meeting by acknowledging all of the amazing success that the company has enjoyed in its early stages, recognizing each of them personally and by name and articulating that each have been critical to the overall potential StrongSpring continues to have as a force in the industry

"But, despite all this success," she says honestly and directly, "as the founder of this organization, I've realized that we've hit a crossroads. If we don't get this issue with the communication between the field reps and home office under control, it's likely we'll be facing rounds of layoffs at best. At worst, we just might lose everything we've all worked so hard to build."

Marley surveys the room. Jane and Norah look stunned, but Charlie, Autumn, and Chloe nod in agreement, appearing to be not at all surprised by the gravity of the situation.

"I didn't ask each of you here today to make you feel that your efforts don't matter and that the company is beyond the point of repair," she says. "I asked you to come together as the most trusted and valuable members of my team to let you know that I've realized something over the past couple of weeks as I've reflected on where we have lost our way a bit as an organization: a *major* factor in this operational slippage is yours truly."

Marley pauses and notices the group leaning forward in their chairs a bit. She certainly has their attention.

"It's been *my* biases toward the ineffective communication between the home office and field operations that have influenced some of the key operational decisions that got us here in the first place. The excuses that I have come up with along the way could fill a dozen whiteboards just like this one I'm standing in front of now. Speaking of this whiteboard, notice up in the top left corner that I've written a series of my own biases—or, in essence, excuses—as to why I believed that our sudden downturn was not a result of internal issues at our home office and instead had everything to do with the areas that each of you in this room oversee."

Marley watches her team digest what's on the whiteboard, their brows furrowing in concentration.

"I'm not asking you to agree with my initial biases," she continues. "But I want to pull back the curtain a bit so that each of you can get a glimpse into how I was originally approaching our operational challenges. I'm not standing here today saying that those biases are correct. In fact, it was when I started to list them on the right side of this whiteboard—or better stated, what I believed to be the biases that field operations held toward the company's overall direction—that I realized two things: (1) All of our supposed 'differences' are much more similar than I originally thought. (See those lines I drew?) (2) And just how dismissive I've been by digging in and anchoring to my own biases and excuses for why our people in the field were unwilling to adapt to what I believed our vision to be."

In case it wasn't obvious before, it's now abundantly clear to the team that this is no regular meeting.

What's Next?

Taking ownership ends when you start taking steps toward turning your differences into similarities, and the next step—*yielding*—starts when you finish sharing your discoveries and ask a core question: "How do you believe we can work toward making progress?" For the first time in this process, you're getting direct input.

And what an exciting and productive place to be!

CHAPTER 7

STEP 5: <u>Y</u>ield

In 2016, my two partners and I created a healthcare company that grew from zero skilled nursing facilities to seventeen in the span of three years. During this period of time, we purchased seven buildings in New Mexico, one of which was in a small town called Aztec, near the city of Farmington. By some strange coincidence, this facility happened to be the place where my grandma spent the last few years of her life before passing away in 2009.

An interesting sidenote is that my grandmother was probably four foot ten, and I'm probably giving her credit for wearing heels the day that measurement was made official. She grew up in a very difficult environment where she had to work all day on her family's ranch just to help make ends meet. Nothing was ever handed to her—not only during her formative years but throughout her life. Legitimately, pound for pound, she was one of the toughest ladies I've ever met (and I know for a fact I'm not alone in that assessment!).

Once, she saw a very rough-looking biker who was having a physical altercation with a woman in the parking lot of a diner. Mollie Bigelow left the diner where she'd been having dinner, approached this giant of a man, and began beating him relentlessly with her large, oversized purse. The biker was a towering man well over six feet tall and more than three hundred pounds, but my grandmother simply didn't care. She wasn't going to leave the woman alone in the parking lot. Mollie Bigelow was a defender of people who were bullied or downtrodden. Due to the obvious size differential and the fact that it was just an incredible "David versus Goliath" story, the incident made the front page of the local newspaper the next day.

While I admired those aspects of her personality, she was never overly touchy-feely with me or any of the other grandkids. She expressed her fondness for others through the principle of tough love. When we assumed operations of the nursing facility where she'd spent her last few years, I was talking to a couple of the women who'd been running the business office when my grandma was there. I said, "You probably don't remember Mollie Bigelow, but . . . " They looked at each other in disbelief. She'd made a huge impression on them, and they started talking about how amazing, inspirational, and kind she was. They saw the spunk and strength but also the tender core. As I listened to them, I could not stop the tears from flowing. It was a blessing to get to see her in a different way through their eyes. After hearing from these kind women in the nursing home, I will never think of my grandmother the same way again. I always loved her and respected her grit, but I hadn't *yielded* to the possibility that she had another side.

Sometimes we give up on people. We assume that even if we resolve the conflict, we'll have to stay guarded and on edge around them for the rest of our lives, because we don't trust they'll be kind to us. It's tempting to believe neither of us can ever truly change, and that conflict resolution is just about checking a box to get business done.

By now, though, you know that's not what UNITY is about. *Yielding* is about turning your heart toward another in an entirely different way.

People are so much more complex and nuanced than we give them credit for. We sometimes think our experience with a person, any person, is definitive—but that's not necessarily the case. There's so much we might not know about someone, and learning more can completely shift our relationship.

That's the beauty of *yielding*.

> ### *Put It into Practice*
>
> *After taking ownership and listening actively, look across the table or desk and ask a very important question: "How do you think we can move forward together?"*

Dual Yielding

Dual yielding is the path forward. What do I mean by that? The goal is for both of you to open up to a mutually beneficial future, not for one of you to submit to the other or drag the other over to your side. Yielding implies consent, willingness, and commitment. Both of you need to see the greater purpose and put the holistic solution above the short-term individual win.

Ideally, you'll begin the UNITY conversation ready and eager to yield, and dual yielding will occur when the other person becomes willing too. When they have the "aha" moment that digging their heels in further is myopic and ultimately self-defeating, they can release the impediments to success that they've been holding on to.

The concept of win-win is simple, but in the heat of a conflict, it takes humility, vulnerability, and time to reach that realization on a practical level. Frequently, the other person needs to take a step back from the meeting to reflect and regroup. Resolution can come from a single conversation, but it most often comes after a series of interactions, punctuated by the necessary time and space.

It's not your role to give the other person assignments between meetings because that wouldn't be an even playing field. The structure of the conversation also isn't "I'm going to tell you how you're wrong, and now you tell me how you'll do things differently." That would, for the lack of a better word, be adversarial.

Curiosity about the other party is rocket fuel for this process. You're there because you genuinely want to understand the other person's perspective, not because you're lobbying to change anyone's mind. Seeking to understand is easier said than done, but that's the frame. I know you have patience and curiosity in you or you wouldn't be trying a new approach to conflict resolution in the first place. If you've prepared yourself mentally and emotionally for the fact that you can't manipulate them, will not force them to agree with you, and may not reach what feels like an ideal resolution, then you can be open to the process and stay focused on learning about the other person and celebrating the changes in yourself.

Dual yielding relates to the self-actualization pinnacle of Maslow's hierarchy of needs. The base of that triangular hierarchy is psychology (food, water, warmth, rest). It then moves up to the next level, which is safety (security and safety needs). Next is social needs (a sense of belonging). Then comes self-esteem (confidence, respect of others, and achievement). And finally, at the apex of Maslow's Pyramid, is self-actualization (morality, creativity, problem solving, acceptance of facts, and lack of prejudice). It is within this high point, where problem solving and acceptance reside, that dual yielding is perpetuated, where it lives and breathes.

In a conflict, the core needs of one person look different from those of another. Most conflict starts on that very first rung, in the psychological frame. People can't get past the idea that their metaphorical food and shelter are more or less important than someone else's—they can't get past the nuts and bolts of the "what" that they've staked their position on. Through UNITY, our goal is to move up the rungs to the higher purpose that unites us.

Ask the Question

When it's time to *yield*, our focus again turns from the "what" to the "why." That's a theme through all the steps, but it's the heart of this one in particular. Your goal is to invite the other person to contribute by asking a question about how they believe the two of you could begin to bridge your differences or make the most progress.

They may come back with ten specific "what" requests: approaches to budgeting, marketing, personnel, you name it. The truth is those are all just byproducts of your common goal: organizational success. One of you might want to invest more in marketing while the other desires more in R & D, but the key point is you both want to grow revenue, build the brand, serve your customers, protect your jobs, and so on. There are a multitude of ways to achieve the same overarching goal, whether that ends up being your idea, their idea, or a new idea that you formulate together.

If you put the ball in their court about moving forward and finding common ground, but they keep coming back to more and more specific "whats" around their position, they may still be in the mindset of your conflict being a zero-sum game. For now, they may believe that in order for them to win, you have to lose.

If so, I suggest reframing with a question to facilitate greater understanding. Ask them, "What are you looking to achieve in your department (or in your family or other arena related to the conflict)? What is your ultimate aim for success?"

Then, just listen. Let them talk it through. It's very important at that point that you concur. Based on what's true for your situation, you might say something like, "Thank you for laying that out. The funny thing is I am looking for the exact same thing, just in a different way." Then, you can explain how all the "whats" you considered in your reflection didn't ultimately relate to the core "why." Setting aside the methods, you're emphasizing that the two of you have the same ultimate aim, which is far more important.

In the example case of marketing versus R & D, you might point out that if they want R & D to be preeminent at the expense of cutting your marketing budget, then it could actually undercut the ultimate aim of company success. If, instead, you find a way for both departments to achieve a win-win, then you can keep collaborating and building each other up, increasing everyone's success over time.

From that perspective, you have a responsibility *to each other* not to cause the other to fail—even just for selfish reasons, because they will help you net greater wins. You don't want to be the reason that the organization turns lopsided and can't maximize its potential because you focused on carving out dominance for yourself at the expense of your colleagues. You now know that path would be unsustainable and lead to a hollow, self-defeating "victory," hobbling the business and creating enemies and animosity.

A better path is one forged in UNITY.

Failing to Yield

The story I'm about to tell you reflects poorly on me, but I look back on it a lot. At the same facility where I did the major reorganization and then launched the Christmas extravaganza, I once terminated a certified nursing assistant—we'll call her Jane—who I believed was engaging in highly self-centered behavior. I've never looked forward to letting someone go so much in my life, but what happened says more about me than her. On her last day, I went to work, knowing she wouldn't be coming back, and I wasn't in a terrible mood as a result, if I'm being totally honest.

Jane had engaged in ongoing negative comments about not just me but operational practices in general and was someone who I described as a bit of a rabble-rouser. I saw her as an employee more interested in sowing chaos than engaging in the important work she was hired to do. She seemed to me to have an agenda, and in my mind, nothing I did could pierce through her general apathy for the company and its people.

Then, she was tardy one day, and another day she didn't give enough notice about not coming in, which technically counted as a "no call, no show." Would that have normally been enough to terminate someone? No. Those two instances might have resulted in a writeup at most. However, I ran with those infractions because of what I believed to be Jane's overall negative impact on facility morale. The moment she made her "no call, no show," I felt like Ed Rooney in *Ferris Bueller's Day Off*, and Jane was Ferris, who wasn't going to get away with anything more under my watch.

That day, I prepared Jane's final check and brought her in.

"You know what?" I said, and then listed all her reasons for termination. "You've been a problem here for a while, Jane, and your recent tardiness and failure to communicate with your supervisor only underscore that point. I'm sorry, but it's just not working out." I figured she'd be dismissive and accusatory right to the end. However, Jane could not have been kinder or more genuine. She was apologetic but also very sincere. She got emotional and had kind things she wanted to say about me and others on the staff.

"I didn't realize that you had this perception of me," she said. "Even though I'm really surprised that I'm being terminated, I respect your ability to put the person you want in that position."

Jane said there was an element of truth in my characterization but also a lack of context. The details she then laid out surrounded her father's failing health and that she was essentially the only person in her household who could take him to his doctor's appointments and frequent urgent care visits. She didn't attempt to justify her tardiness or the fact that when she didn't call in soon enough, it was because she was with her father at the hospital listening to doctors and nurses explain the many complexities of his illness. She also told me that she'd had a bad experience at a prior company where management had mistreated her. She admitted to warning a couple of people at our facility to be cautious about trusting management, but she wasn't trying to undermine the operation. By the end of our conversation, she could not have been more gracious, sincere, and honest. I saw her through a different set of eyes on that day.

After she left, I talked to her immediate supervisor and expressed my surprise at how the conversation had gone. The supervisor said, "Why would it surprise you? She's my best worker. She is the most amazing person on the floor."

In that moment, I realized the whole series of events had been "The Brandon Show." Everything I'd done was about how *I* felt, how *I* saw what *I* wanted to see, how *I* got angry that she was not meeting *my* needs, and how *I* viewed her as a threat. In reality, Jane was a well-respected employee. She could have been an ally, and she may have had legitimate concerns that could've benefitted our facility. And without question, one of the worst things about my mistake was that

I didn't talk to Jane or her supervisor before firing her. I blindly followed my own misguided view of Jane and her motivations. I allowed my misperceptions to cloud my view of the great employee and great human being that Jane truly was and is to this day.

A week after I talked to her supervisor, I called Jane to ask how her job search was going. She said that she had some solid prospects but nothing had come through yet. After a bit more chitchat, I mustered up the courage to ask Jane what had been on my mind since the day I let her go. "Jane, this question may surprise you, but I wanted to find out if you'd consider giving us another shot?"

She was understandably confused. And as she continued to ask questions, it was clear that I needed to provide her some context and assurance.

"Well," I told her, "I just want you to know your termination didn't come from the company or the other managers. It was all me. I made a lot of really bad assumptions about you, and I just wanted to apologize. Based upon the things that I said to you as we parted, I wouldn't blame you if you didn't want to consider coming back. But would you ever consider giving me a second chance?" I told her about all the people who defended her and that I'd failed in listening to their views and opinions of her work and character. I confessed to her that this was far from my proudest moment. I told her I was ashamed, and that I would consider it the greatest honor if she would contemplate returning, with a healthy pay increase of course.

Jane did indeed return—and not only did we develop a positive working relationship, but we became good friends.

Seeing the Bigger Picture

Within a year of that experience, I had to let go of another employee for financial reasons. The leadership asked me to clean house. I'll never forget one of the women I chose to let go. I told her, "I'm so sorry this isn't working out. It has nothing to do with you. We're just making changes."

For the next ten minutes, she was so gracious. I should have done my homework, because I later found out she was one of the best people at her role. She could have laid into me and asked, "Are you kidding? Do you know how much money I've saved the company by doing X, Y, and Z?" Maybe she should have stood up for herself in that moment, but she just had amazing humility and poise.

Based on her conduct, I ended up ripping up the termination check and told her, "Financially, I don't know how I'm going to make this work, but you are the kind of person that embodies the culture that we want to create."

She became a leader and a mentor for all the other nurses who were training to promote into the higher-level position that she was currently occupying at the time. We made her a head of culture development for the nursing division because of that one interaction.

In both cases, I hadn't unpacked and navigated before entering the conversation. I was so stuck on my own selfish wants, needs, and distorted sense of reality, that I couldn't see the bigger picture staring right back at me. In trying to save money, I was penny-wise and pound-foolish. Once I looked into the eyes and saw the soul of a person who was right for the job and could enhance our mission, I knew that keeping her on would increase our financial success in the long term. It's a great reminder that when we stop viewing people as impediments and start recognizing them as foundational to our success, the synergy we truly seek will finally, after long last, be discovered.

It's very human to jump straight to logistics without doing our research. It's admirable to want to protect your business and your team. You have full permission to make mistakes, learn, and grow. But there are consequences and missed opportunities when you fail to recognize the full humanity and potential of the people in front of you.

Yielding Is for Companies, Too

Once, my company worked with a group at a medical facility where an employee had gone to HR with accusations of favoritism and being passed over for a promotion. Those complaints are not uncommon. Nothing had yet escalated to legal action. HR took the step of talking to that individual before speaking to their supervisor. That particular supervisor explained the decision as being based on "choosing people who had a greater combination of education and experience." The process sounded legitimate, and HR followed up with the complainant to explain the outcome of the investigation. The complainant didn't appear happy, but she seemed to move on.

Two months later, though, she claimed verbal harassment and that she'd been given assignments and tasks that others weren't asked to perform. HR opened a new investigation but couldn't find any proof or corroboration of the allegations. Once again, HR followed up with the complainant to explain the outcome of their findings.

Four months later, this same employee resigned from the company, hired an attorney, and made an allegation of wrongful termination. As it turned out, the case never made it to court. Instead, it went to arbitration. The arbitrator in the case found that although HR had witnessed and represented the employee as having an ax to grind, there actually was substantiation of her claims, and the employer-led investigations had been insufficient. The accusations were not substantiated at the time because the investigators failed to ask the right questions. They didn't actually talk to the right people who could've shed much greater light on this particular circumstance. Plus, there was a cover-up involving important emails that would have supported the complainant's case that were intentionally deleted and wiped from the server.

On the surface, the employee seemed like she was "crying wolf." In practice, HR wasn't getting to the bottom of real issues. During the course of the investigation, the attorneys were able to pull deleted emails and other digital evidence that showed the employee was, in fact, correct all along.

The *yielding* portion came during the arbitration process, when the owners of the company and the COO, who hadn't known about the cover-up, discovered that they had misinterpreted the situation due to their own lack of awareness of the nefarious things happening right underneath their noses. They were suddenly and dramatically seeing this employee through a totally different lens, and these heads of the company realized that *they* were actually the problem.

At that stage of the legal process, they had a choice. They could have agreed to a hefty settlement through a prepared nondisclosure agreement in exchange for the employee to acknowledge the company did nothing wrong. Instead, they did something amazing. They offered a sizeable amount on top of an already agreed-to payment, specifically adding an "emotional distress" clause that had not been in the agreement when it was first drafted. This additional payment was not demanded by the former employee in this case, but rather the company as an acknowledgment of something that shouldn't have happened but unfortunately did. In all my years, I've never directly witnessed or heard of any case where additional money was offered by defendant's counsel AFTER both sides had already come to terms with an agreement that all parties were happy with.

Then, as if that financial gesture wasn't proof enough of a change of heart that occurred with ownership, they offered to bring the employee back as the assistant HR director. She'd now be in charge of employee engagement and earn a salary that was nearly triple what she had previously made. Responsibilities of the role would include double-checking HR investigations to ensure employees' perspectives were represented, not just managers' perspectives. The company created a situation in which the employee not only received compensation but also recognition for standing her ground—and to the happy ending we go . . . the employee gleefully accepted this generous and impressive offer.

I've never seen such a stark example of dual yielding. It went from an extremely contentious preparation process for litigation to the complainant actually returning to the company that admitted wrongdoing in order to make it better. Despite all the initial hard feelings, the adversaries became collaborators, and the company recognized the accuser as a valuable asset. That's the pinnacle of Maslow's hierarchy. The complainant could have taken the money and split, just focusing on survival, but instead, she embarked on a new, higher purpose. Had she pursued the complaint to court, she might have gotten even more money and even tanked the company, but she realized she could achieve something more meaningful, with greater peace of mind, by returning to the team.

Nothing about this instance was about getting the upper hand or forcing someone into submission. Both sides changed.

When my company began working with our client after the arbitration, I was there to help them ensure they never regressed to the previous culture and way of doing business. They'd already done the hard work, and I helped them formalize that self-awareness. Usually, we're involved in the throes of really terrible things, but in that case, we just did some maintenance work, which speaks to how evolved that company really was—and how powerful dual yielding is.

The lesson? At its heart, UNITY shows us that we can be better because of what we discover about ourselves.

Common Pitfalls and Pushbacks When Yielding

When you enter in the fifth and final step of UNITY, you are likely to be enthusiastic and excited about moving to resolution (or, at the very least, understanding). After all, you're highly motivated since you'll have done all the work in the prior steps, and odds are you're ready to embrace a new normal that's more peaceful and harmonious.

Wonderful! But here's a caveat that can become a pitfall if you aren't aware: just because you have done the work and are ready, that does not mean others will be quite there yet. UNITY is meant to be followed genuinely and with intention but at no point does it involve manipulating or coercing other parties. Remember, there is no "winning" here . . . there is only coming together.

If you find yourself frustrated by a lack of buy-in or an outcome that wasn't what you had in mind, I challenge you to reassess your definition of success. This point brings up a memory for me: If I close my eyes, I can still hear a coach from my football years yelling, "Bigelow! Control what you can control! You're the safety. Don't worry about the D-line, the linebackers, or the defensive backs. You have your assignment! Do it to the best of your ability and stop worrying about everybody else, or we'll find someone who can."

While a little harsh, he was right. And, like most good advice, that lesson stands today, too. Even if you follow every step of UNITY to the letter, you may be the only one who changes, and the conflict may not come to a resolution. However, I'll bet you will not approach conflict the same way ever again, after you've learned to bring both sides to the table within an emotional narrative that has the potential to profoundly change perspectives and bring better, more connected outcomes.

And even though the goal of UNITY is not to win, winning is clearly an important outcome.

Put It into Practice

No matter the outcome of the yielding, take care to celebrate your growth through completing the UNITY process.

At its heart, UNITY shows us that we can be better because of what we discover about ourselves and others.

UNITY in Action: StrongSpring Yields

At this point in her meeting with her company brain trust, Marley has shown her ability to own and communicate her role in StrongSpring's unhealthy culture. She has also revealed to her management team her ability to thoughtfully consider and invest the time necessary to prioritize the expectations, frustrations, and viewpoints that are being felt throughout the organization. This opens the door to a new and profound approach—one being adopted in real time from the very top.

After Marley relates to the group her part in this systemwide problem, it's time to *yield* to new possibilities. Marley begins with Chloe, asking her three questions:

1 "How are you feeling right now?"
2 "How can you help ensure that we all meet in the future the moment this kind of division creeps in?"
3 "How do we ensure as leadership that we'll always *yield* to possibilities to improve communication at *all levels*?"

Marley writes down Chloe's responses on the whiteboard. One by one, she repeats this exercise with each of the other executives. Marley then compares and contrasts all of the responses that were provided, and together, the group begins to whiteboard a plan.

What's Next?

Through UNITY, I've learned not to fault people I'm in conflict with, regardless of the outcome of the *yield* phase. Instead, I respect them because they feel so strongly about a position, even if it's different from mine. Those dynamics are still challenging, but they also expand my point of view and my options. There's a huge part of me that loves running up against that passion in people I'm in conflict with because I know they aren't apathetic. If I never disagree with someone, then it's usually because they don't have strong opinions and don't care. In the long run, that lack of interest is harder to work with. Give me the passion, any day.

In that way—and many others—conflict is healthy. It is the impetus for change, for connection, for empathy . . . if we only allow it to be.

Unity and Beyond: Where We Go from Here

n July of 1982, my family took a summer trip to Idaho Falls to visit my cousins. I was so excited! One of the events that was planned was a river rafting excursion on the Snake River, which ran very close to where my cousins lived.

On that beautiful summer day as we departed from shore in a six-person raft, I was joined by my father, uncle, grandfather, and cousin. After a wonderful day on the water, as we looked to take the raft to shore, we kept looking away from the river to try to spot our cars on shore. What we couldn't have possibly known at the time was what began as a Keystone Cop's exercise—each of us believing we spotted our cars along the shore, only to be proven wrong each step of the way—turned into a near-tragedy of astronomical proportions.

Amid our distraction and confusion about where to take the raft to shore, we suddenly jerked forward, pulled by an intensely powerful force. It was a large whirlpool, lying in wait, that was directly in front of a large concrete dam. Immediately we all began to violently thrash the boat's paddles, in all directions, in an effort to reverse course away from imminent doom. Unfortunately, our efforts proved futile. Within seconds, the whirlpool yanked the boat, and each of us, into this watery vortex forty feet below.

As we all went under, the boat was the last to succumb and was immediately torn apart. Pieces of it shot through a large feeder gate and into the great unknown. Fortunately for each of us, we weren't immediately shredded into a thousand pieces. However, we were jerked in all directions and churned round and round at the bottom of the Snake River for close to sixty seconds before catching a massive gush of water that miraculously propelled us through a huge tunnel. Then, at the moment we realized we were not long for this world, we were hurled into the light and down into the swift moving river below.

Relief turned back into panic when we realized we were in the middle of the raging river with a powerful undertow, sharp rocks, and dangerous branches all around us. Because we were all in the deep throws of the "fight or flight" adrenaline response, we had no idea of the extent of our injuries or levels of fatigue. We would eventually discover the answer to those mysteries, but first we had to, one by one, find our way to shore.

Sitting here today, over four decades removed from one of the most horrific and life-altering experiences of my life, I can't actually say how each of us in our tattered and broken conditions made it to shore in those rapid moving currents. I also can't adequately explain one of the greatest mysteries of all that July day on the Snake River. We discovered, as each of us somehow made it to shore, that an ambulance was called. The deputy sheriff arrived within minutes after the accident.

I don't remember a lot from that day, but I do vividly recall what this man said as we all were finally reunited along the banks, grateful to be alive. He called it "an absolute miracle!" He explained that over a recent five-week period, two different groups of people in rafts just like ours had been killed. Eight rafters total had lost their lives in that same awful whirlpool.

It's hard to describe and analyze what the impact of this watershed moment was in my very young life. Ultimately, I believe that it set the stage as my brain continued to fully form that I may . . . just may . . . have been put on this earth for a purpose. And just maybe, that purpose had something to do with aiding others in overcoming obstacles, challenges, and trauma in their lives.

For me, that way has been UNITY.

UNITY in Action: StrongSpring's Bright Future

Marley and her management team work together to whiteboard the following plan of action, one not only to address the problem at hand but also to make sure this dynamic doesn't ever repeat:

- Chloe will be in charge of calendaring, inviting, and ensuring that a quarterly UNITY meeting happens, in person, with this group.
- Charlie will take charge of putting together a quarterly survey of employees regarding home office/field ops communications and how it can be improved. He is tasked with bringing those results to the new quarterly meetings.
- Jane will have oversight of ensuring that all of the field managers follow up with and complete these quarterly surveys.
- Autumn will own a critical step: ensuring the accurate and timely delivery of these results back to Norah.
- Norah's oversight will include analyzing trends in quarterly responses and sharing those findings at an annual executive retreat now planned for each fall.

Marley smiles, pleased to see her team come together in such a beautiful way. She knows the key with this entirely new frontier that she initiated can be summed up in one sentence: The executive leadership team is holding itself accountable and inviting the entire company to view their professional relationships and responsibilities through a lens of UNITY—a new way of seeing, approaching, and solving problems now and in the future.

Being the Change

At the end of the day, UNITY aims to find a harmonious relationship with people we're in conflict with. If that's not possible in the present because they're not ready, then UNITY lays the groundwork for developing a complete understanding of what it will take to have strong, symbiotic relationships well into in the future. It provides a pathway for tackling the conflict in front of you while also stoking a synergy that helps root out and prevent future conflicts, and—last but certainly not least—it's simply a more peaceful way to live. Sign me up for that seven ways to Sunday and twice on Tuesdays!

The secret sauce for this process is finding a way to be humble but not passive. UNITY is for people who are tired of constantly fighting with others and then rushing into temporary solutions in the interest of profitability, efficiency, or appeasing their boss. UNITY is about a true change of heart and mind that moves you forward in a new way.

In fact, we've found that people who truly embrace this method have fewer conflicts in general. They learn to take other perspectives and preemptively find common ground instead of needing to clean up messes after the fact. The conflicts don't completely go away, but their approach to the people around them changes.

I love the UNITY process because it's beautiful to witness as it unfolds. Suddenly there's collaboration that never could have existed before, and moving forward, it prevents new conflicts from penetrating every aspect of personal and professional lives.

Conversation precedes conflict, and you can stop there if you know how to have one productively. The impact ripples outward because once you positively alter a relationship with someone, they too can see the possibility of transformative resolution. Whether you work together or are members of the same family, now you're both yielding to new possibilities with each other and with other people in your lives. You've become part of a "we" with greater meaning and purpose. You're on the same side instead of divided by conflict, and that's when the synergy of one plus one equals five can take hold.

You're a unified force, and together, you can approach future challenges more effectively than you ever could divided and alone.

I encourage you to practice UNITY in your own life and see the results for yourself. You can find further information, as well as many other resources that will help you in your own journey for a life full of optimism and clarity. UNITY provides the tools to not just resolve conflict, but to know the signs and symptoms as they creep into your organizational, personal, and family relationships now and well into the future. Head to https://www.fusionconflictstrategies.com.

What's Next?

The most successful processes are truly life-changing because they involve not just an intellectual breakthrough but also a genuine, shared emotional connection. Through the UNITY framework, I've seen people who were previously in conflict hug, cry, and apologize in front of dozens of their colleagues, pledging to approach the relationship in a new way moving forward. Of course, they still have issues and differences at times, but they finally have a powerful understanding of where the other person is actually coming from.

And what comes next? I believe what the *world needs now* is not only *love sweet love* . . . but also an entirely new way forward. UNITY will help you begin that journey TODAY!

ABOUT THE AUTHOR

Brandon Bigelow has spent the better part of nearly thirty years in pursuit of resolving conflict at all levels of organizations. The majority of that time involved a multitude of healthcare organizations in operations, strategic planning, HR, risk management, and employment-related dispute matters. Over the course of his career, Brandon has taken a keen interest in developing positive, accountable organizations and has established numerous conflict resolution processes and tools that have allowed leaders and corporate executives to reduce organizational risk, manage internal disputes, reduce legal costs, and create systemic accountability.

Brandon began his career as a healthcare administrator in 1997. He managed post-acute care operations, and in addition to consistently achieving financial and clinical results that exceeded company, state, and federal expectations, his focus was first and foremost on stabilizing and inspiring employees and organizations in culture change. Brandon continued his upward trajectory within healthcare and led several organizations as head of business development, VP of mergers and acquisitions, regional director of operations, and senior VP of operations.

During his career, he also founded three companies. His healthcare business eventually grew to 1,700 employees and over $100 million in annual revenues. At his own companies, and while working for others, Brandon always instilled innovative organizational dispute resolution programs. As a result, he set industry standards for retention and employee-related claims, and he drove drastic reductions in overall legal expenses.

Brandon studied political science and economics and received a bachelor's degree from the University of Utah. He continued his education and earned a master of public administration (MPA) from California State University, Fresno. His legal education followed, and he earned a master of dispute resolution (MDR) from the Rick J. Caruso School of Law at Pepperdine University.

Learn more about Brandon and his work at:
https://www.fusionconflictstrategies.com.

ACKNOWLEDGMENTS

Kathryn, I still want to be YOU when I grow up! I have a long way to go to achieve that, but your insistence on pushing yourself to be the best version of you, no matter what you do in life, inspired me to pour myself into this work. You're my person, my very best friend, and the one for whom I will still gladly be doing "soda runs" (five minutes before the mini-mart closes) when we're in our nineties . . . I love you WAY more than I can say!

An acknowledgment is inadequate, but nevertheless, I simply must express an overwhelming amount of gratitude for the guiding influence and steady hand of my dear mother, Vicki Bigelow. Though the awful grip of Alzheimer's has robbed you of so much, you are still the quintessential peacemaker. You inspired the very foundation of the UNITY framework! Mom, I sure wish you could read this book. I have no doubt your suggestions and input would've made it even better. I love you always and forever!

Dad, thank you from the bottom of my heart for ensuring that I never just settled in life. You showed me, through your love and confidence in me, that eventually that naive twelve-year-old who backed your brand-new car into a fire hydrant would pull it together and maybe even have something meaningful to offer this world. I can never thank you enough for this deeply impactful and meaningful gift. But of course, the greatest lesson of all has been your love, devotion, and attention to the woman who gave me life. There cannot be a more unselfish, Christlike example of what true love means than what I witness from you on a daily basis. I love you, Dad!

To each of my six children (Corinne, Jared, Will, Natalie, Camille, and Reid), sons-in-law (Sam and Luke), daughter-in-law (Whitney), and six grandchildren (and leaders within StrongSpring—bonus points if you figured that out earlier in the book—Marley, Jane, Norah, Charlie, Autumn, and Chloe): you are my reason for existing. My pride in who each of you are today is only matched by my confidence in the endless capacity that you bring the world tomorrow!

To my editor extraordinaire, Jessica Burdg; your confidence in me and relentless pursuit to discover the essence of what conflict is truly all about is a testament to your brilliance as a pure storyteller. Your innate ability to draw from me what I literally didn't know was there is truly something to behold, and I will forever be grateful. This book would not have made it to the finish line without your guiding influence . . . you're simply the best!

I wish to thank deeply my professional muse, partner in business, and friend for life, Nicole Redstone. Your steadiness "at the wheel" and your ability to develop deep and meaningful relationships on levels most people can only dream of is something to behold!

Thank you to Liz Vindiola for your willingness to take a chance on a dream, inspire people, and remedy and root out conflict wherever it lies! Who would've known our time together at Pepperdine would've led to such a beautiful partnership and collaboration?! You will always be my "go-to" when I struggle for the next great idea and when the ever-elusive "light bulb moment" is just around the bend!

I'd like to acknowledge and express my deep gratitude to my dear friend and one of my professional mentors, Julianne Williams. Your knowledge and skill in the healthcare operating space is only surpassed by your incredibly empathic perspectives to those who grieve and mourn. You're one of the strongest people I know, and your life story of achievement and overcoming obstacles should be a case study for those looking for guidance and inspiration from someone who's lived and breathed true empowerment and been courageous enough to share that story with the world!

Thank you to all of those who constantly inspire me, including you, Jazmin Vazquez. Learning your story of immigrating to this country and working to support your family—all while centering positivity and growth even in the face of seemingly insurmountable challenges and odds—is a shining example of *yielding* to new possibilities and the importance of not making assumptions. Your work to achieve your BSN and ultimately as a nurse practitioner, considering all you've had to overcome, is impressive beyond words! I am grateful that we get to work together and that I get to continue to be astonished by all the things you do.

Thank you, thank you, thank you, team Dinuba! You know who you are, but you may never know just how much you inspired me to follow my passion, even when reality slapped me in the face time and time and time again!

www.ingramcontent.com/pod-product-compliance
Lightning Source LLC
Chambersburg PA
CBHW030521210326
41597CB00013B/983